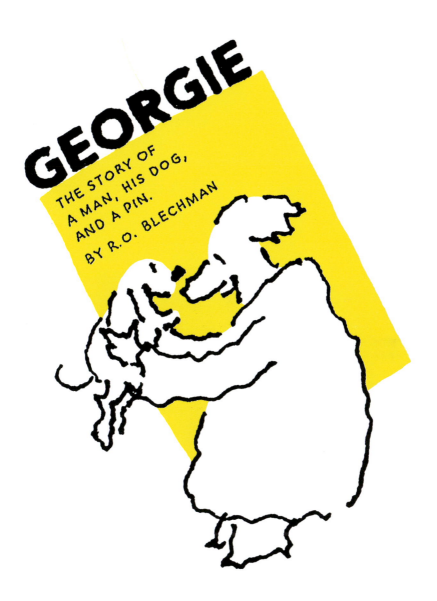

GEORGIE

THE STORY OF A MAN, HIS DOG, AND A PIN.
BY R.O. BLECHMAN

DOVER PUBLICATIONS, INC.
Mineola, New York

Bibliographical Note

This Dover edition, first published in 2016, is a republication of the text and illustrations from *Georgie*: *The Story of a Man, His Dog, and a Pin*, originally published in *Talking Lines: The Graphic Stories of R. O. Blechman*, by Drawn & Quarterly, Montreal, in 2009.

Library of Congress Cataloging-in-Publication Data

Names: Blechman, R. O. (Robert O.), 1930–author, illustrator.
Title: Georgie : the story of a man, his dog, and a pin / R. O. Blechman.
Description: Mineola, New York : Dover Publications, 2016.
Identifiers: LCCN 2016013081| ISBN 9780486808864 | ISBN 0486808866
Subjects: LCSH: Graphic novels.

Classification: LCC PN6733.B54 G46 2016 | DDC 741.5/973—dc23 LC record available at http://lccn.loc.gov/2016013081

Manufactured in China by RR Donnelley
80886601   2016
www.doverpublications.com

GEORGIE

I once read of a dog who was taught a few words (although maybe I dreamed this up). Anyway, it inspired me to write this piece. Its genesis, probably, also had something to do with the birth of my first son and all the anxieties that new fatherhood entailed.

It was like an appletree in winter...

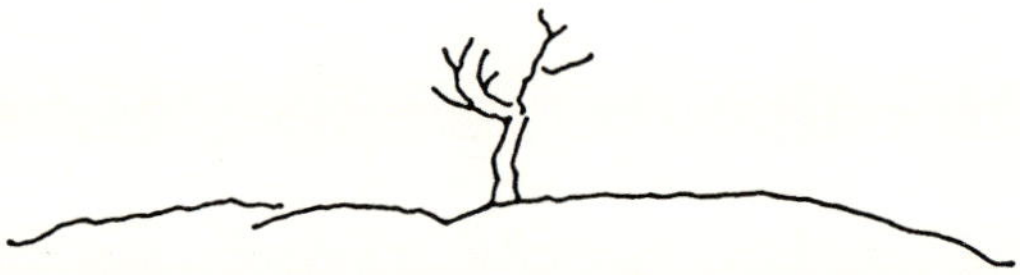

...suddenly bearing fruit.

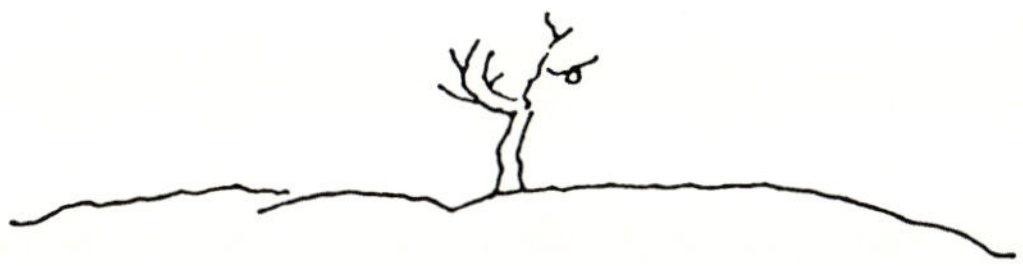

Minnie Goodwin had a baby.

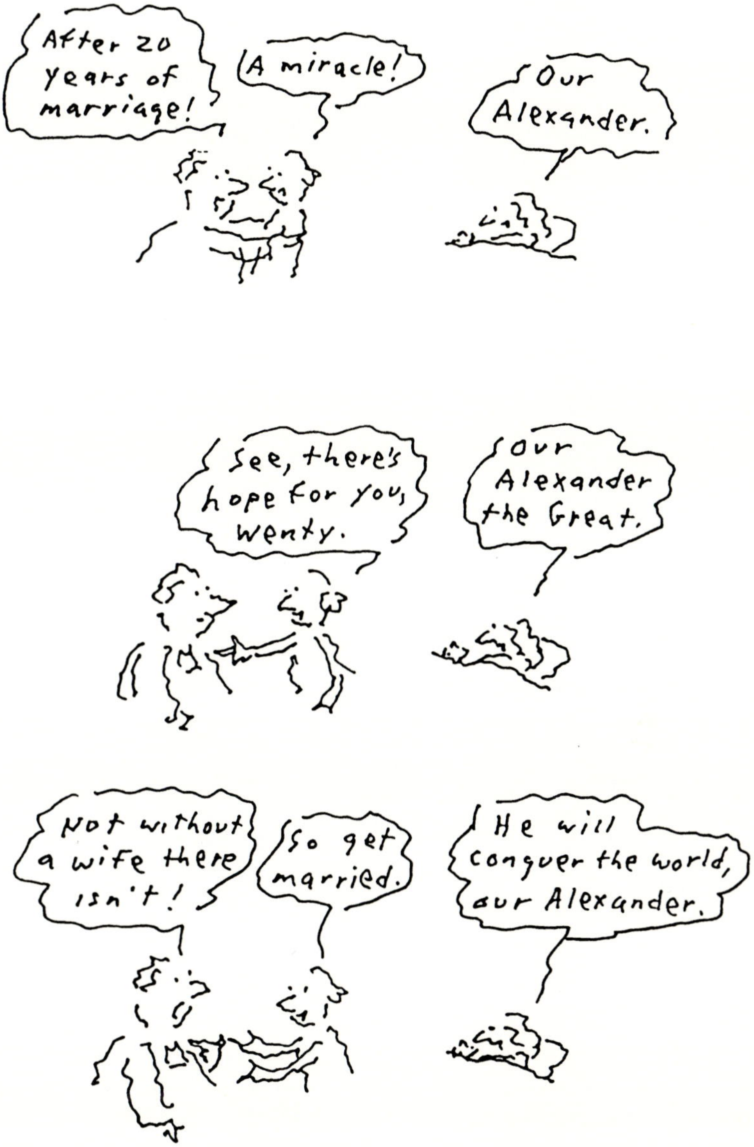
After 20 years of marriage!
A miracle!
Our Alexander.
See, there's hope for you, Wenty.
Our Alexander the Great.
Not without a wife there isn't!
So get married.
He will conquer the world, our Alexander.

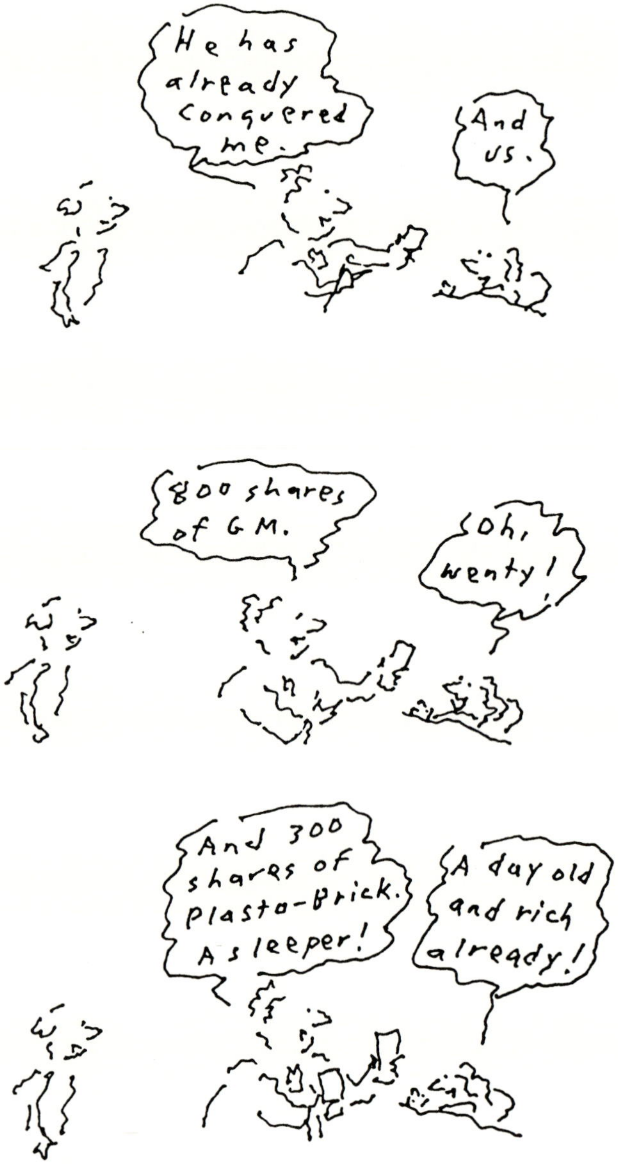
He has already conquered me.
And us.
800 shares of GM.
Oh, wenty!
And 300 shares of plasto-Brick. A sleeper!
A day old and rich already!

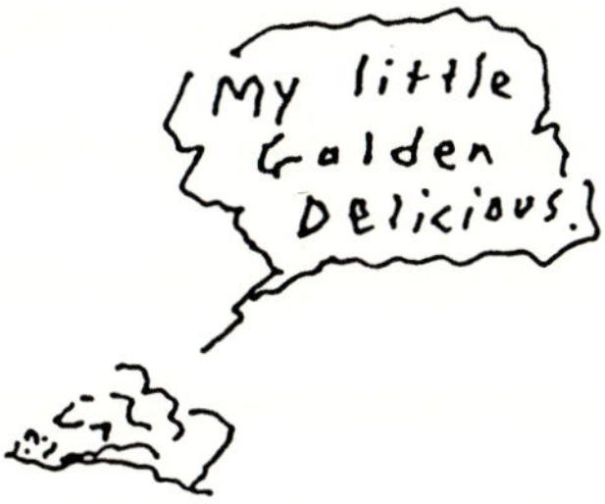
My little Golden Delicious.

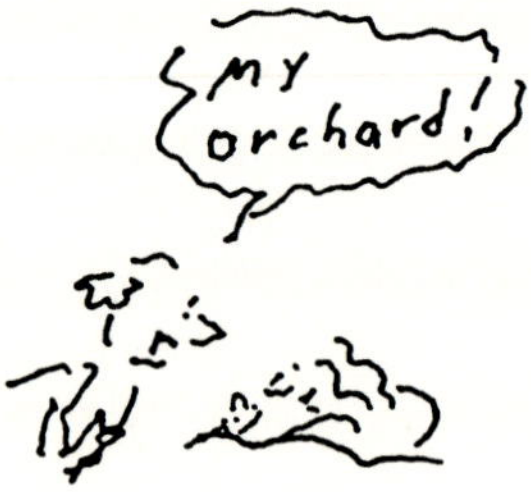
my orchard!

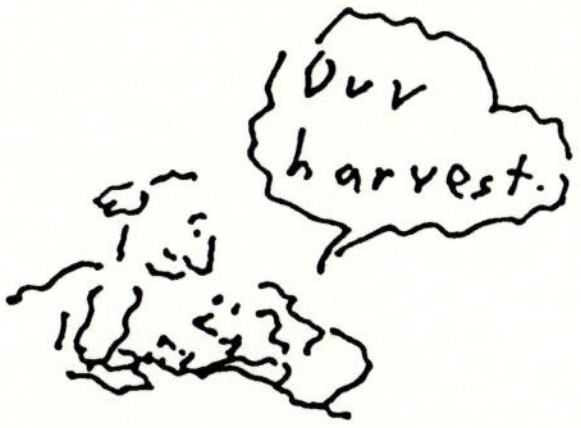
Our harvest.

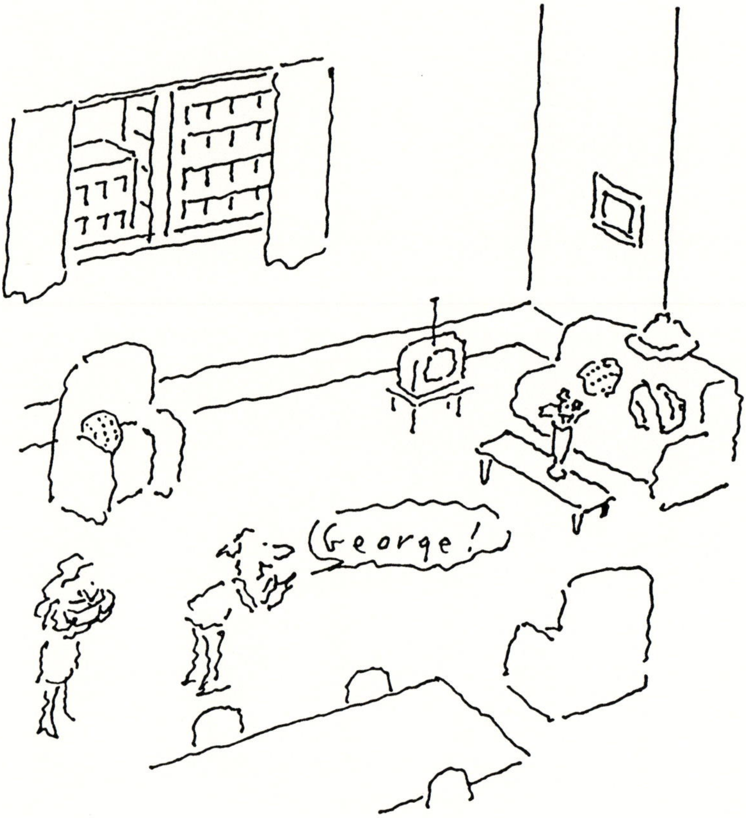
George!

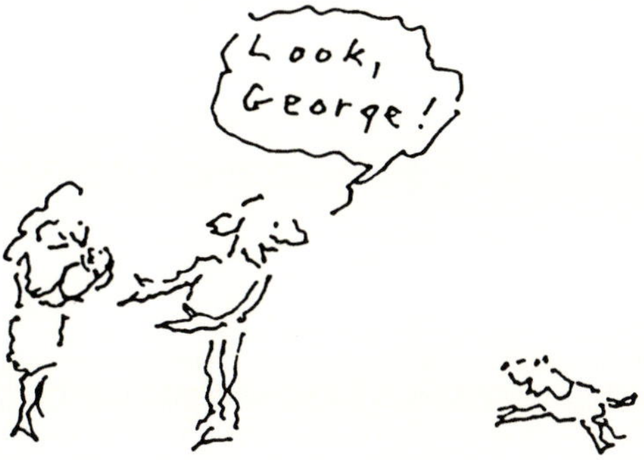
Look, George!

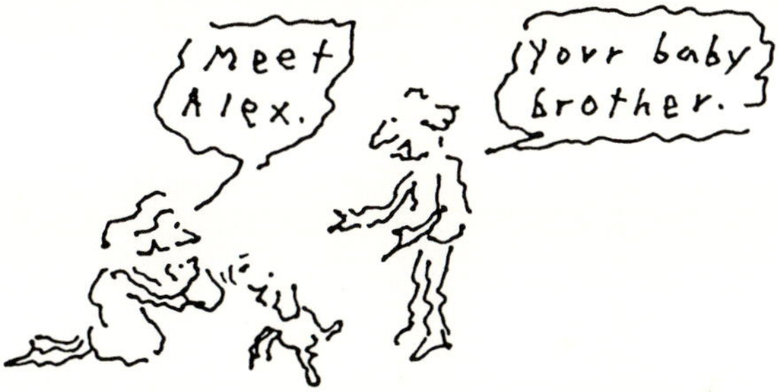
Meet Alex.
Your baby brother.

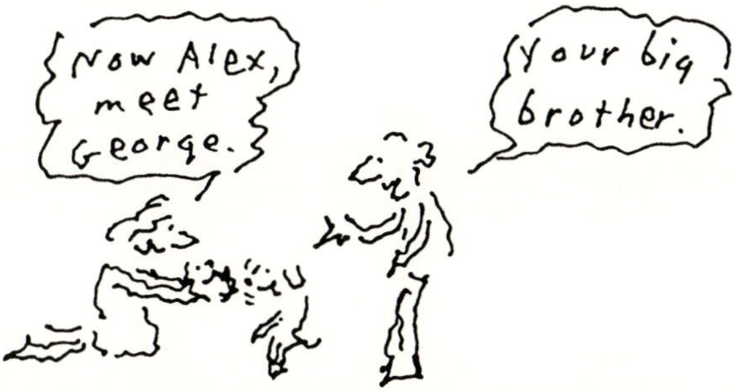
Now Alex, meet George.
Your big brother.

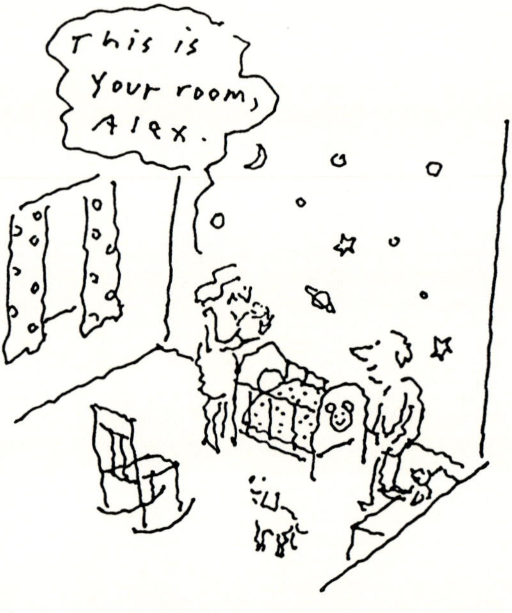
This is your room, Alex.

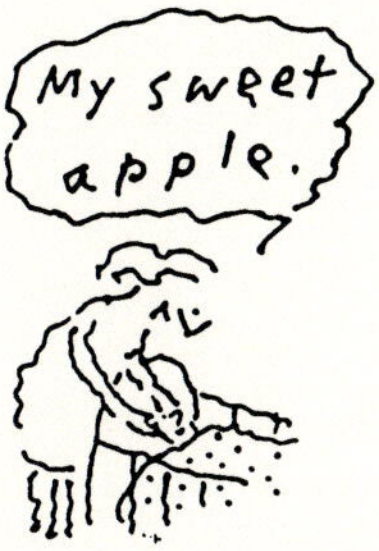
My sweet apple.

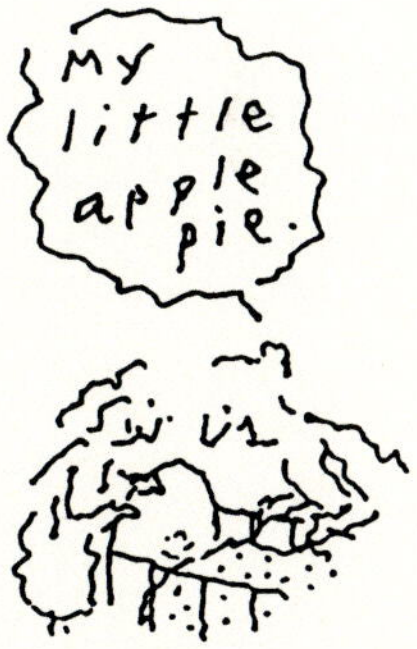
My little apple pie.

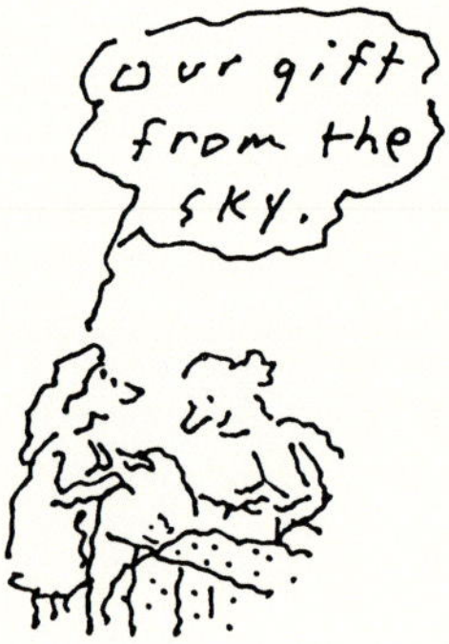
our gift from the sky.

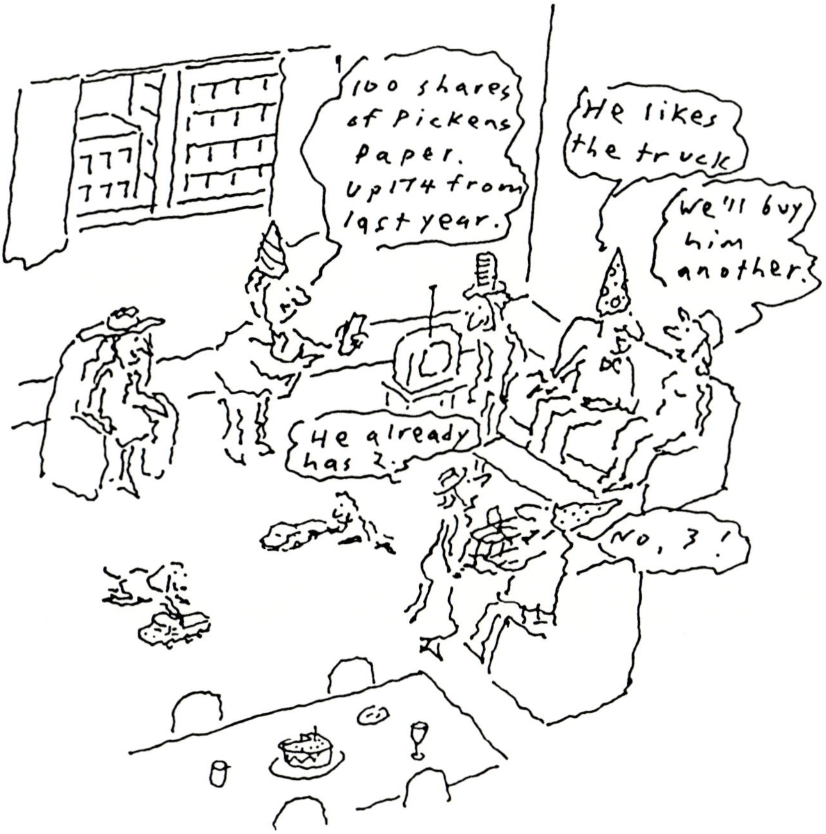
100 shares of Pickens paper. Up 174 from last year.
He likes the truck
We'll buy him another.
He already has 2.
No, 3!

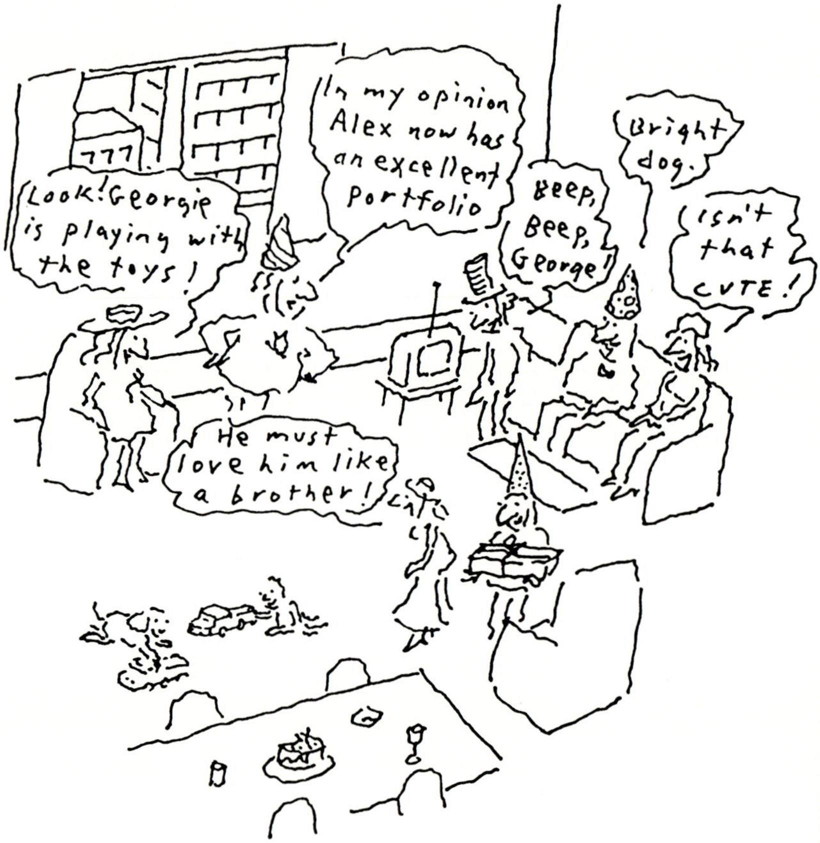
Look! Georgie is playing with the toys!
In my opinion Alex now has an excellent Portfolio
Beep, Beep, George!
Bright dog.
isn't that CUTE!
He must love him like a brother!

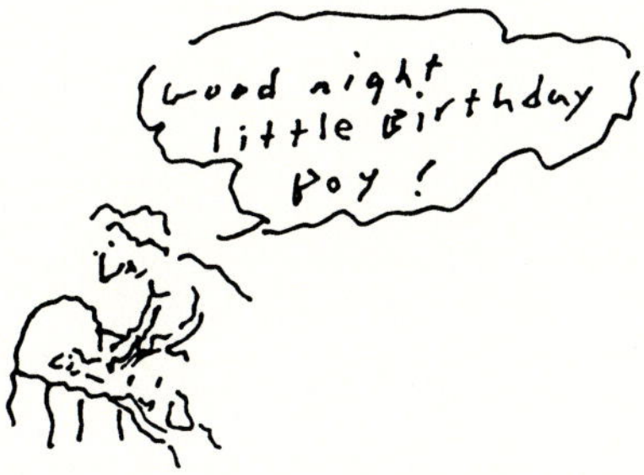
Good night little Birthday Boy!

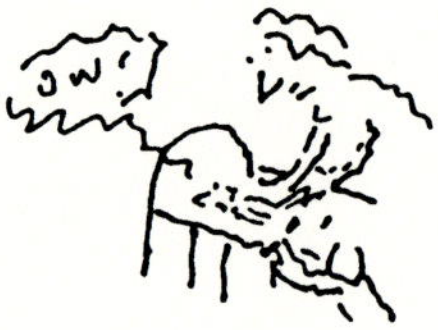
OW!

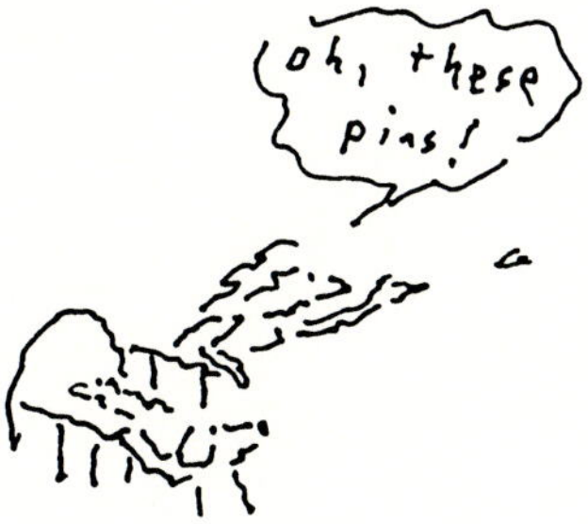
Oh, these pins!

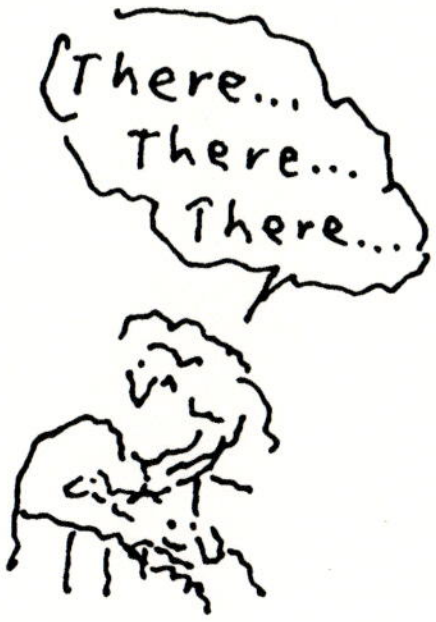
There... There... There...

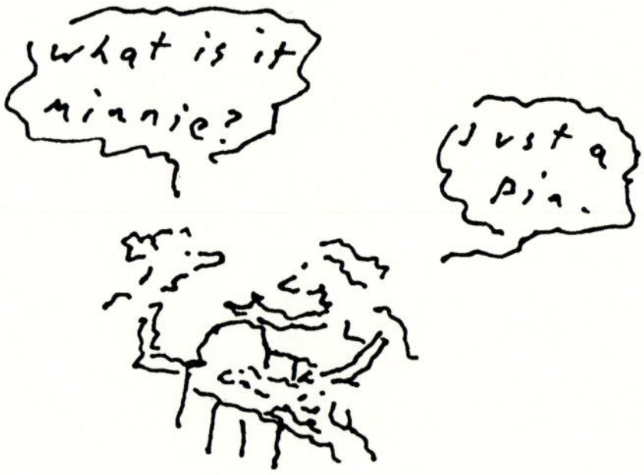
what is it minnie?
Just a pin.

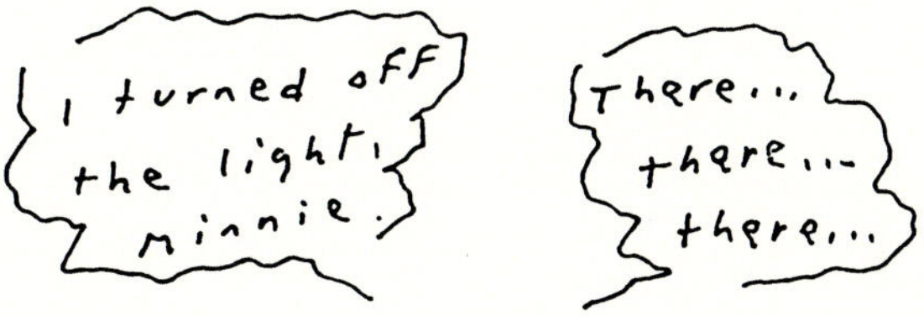
I turned off the light, Minnie.
There... there... there...

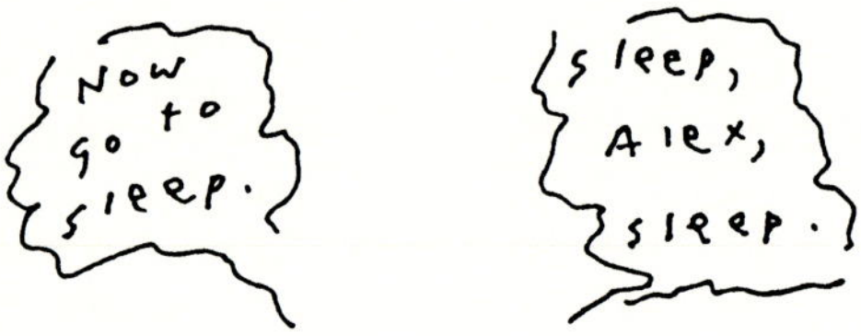
Now go to sleep.
sleep, Alex, sleep.

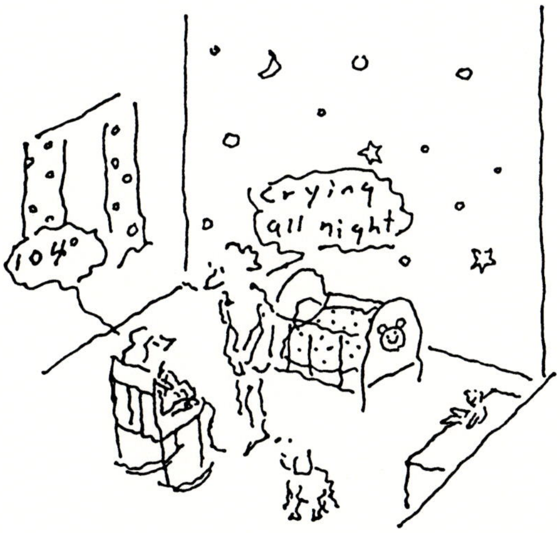
104°
crying
all night

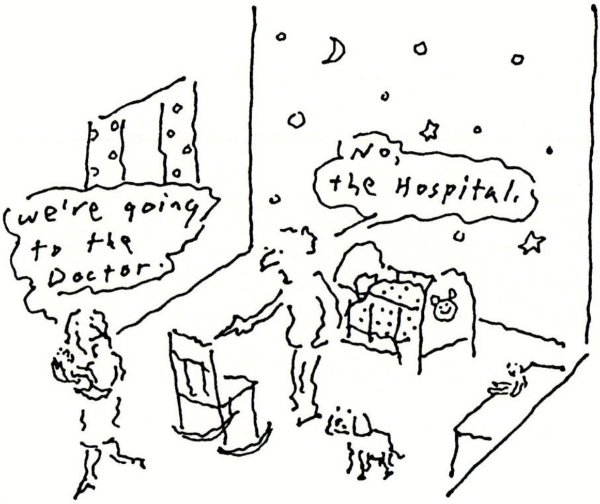
we're going to the Doctor.
No, the Hospital.

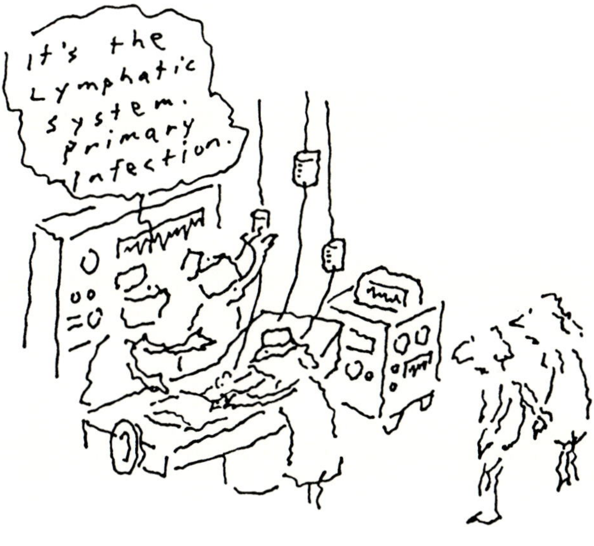
It's the Lymphatic system. primary infection.

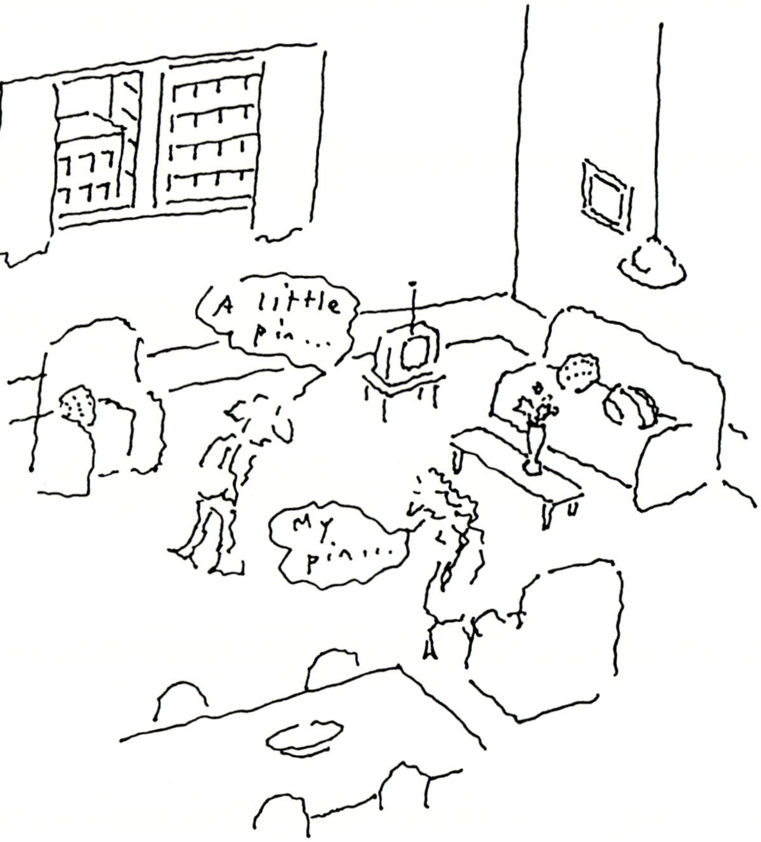
A little pin...
My pin...

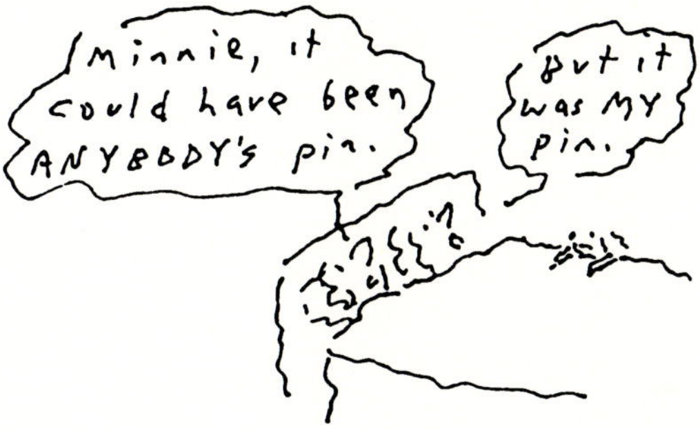
Minnie, it could have been ANYBODY'S pin.
But it was MY pin.

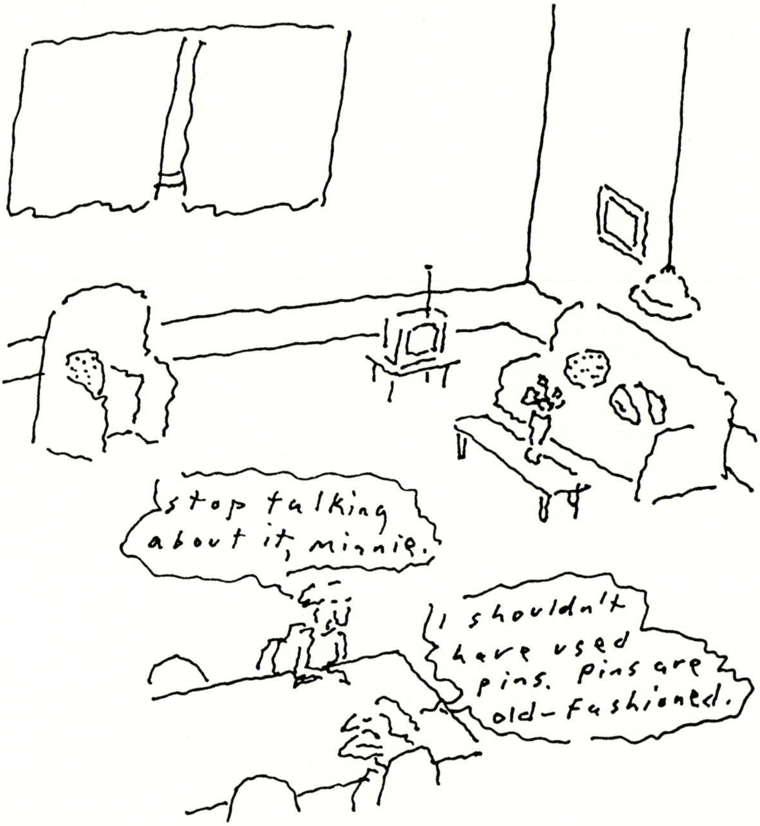
stop talking about it, minnie.
I shouldn't have used pins. Pins are old-fashioned.

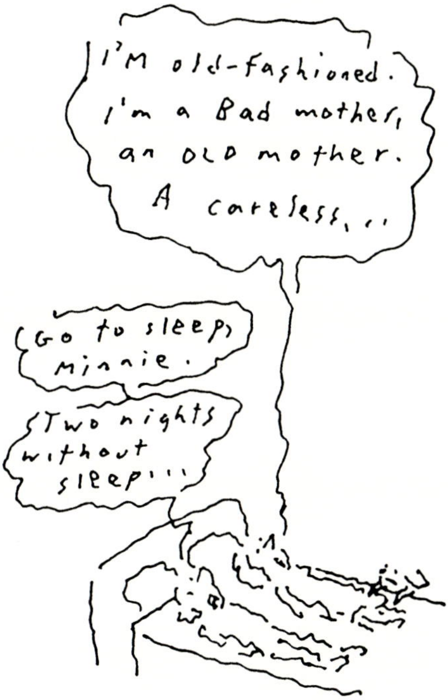
I'M old-fashioned. I'm a Bad mother, an OLD mother. A careless...
Go to sleep, minnie.
Two nights without sleep...

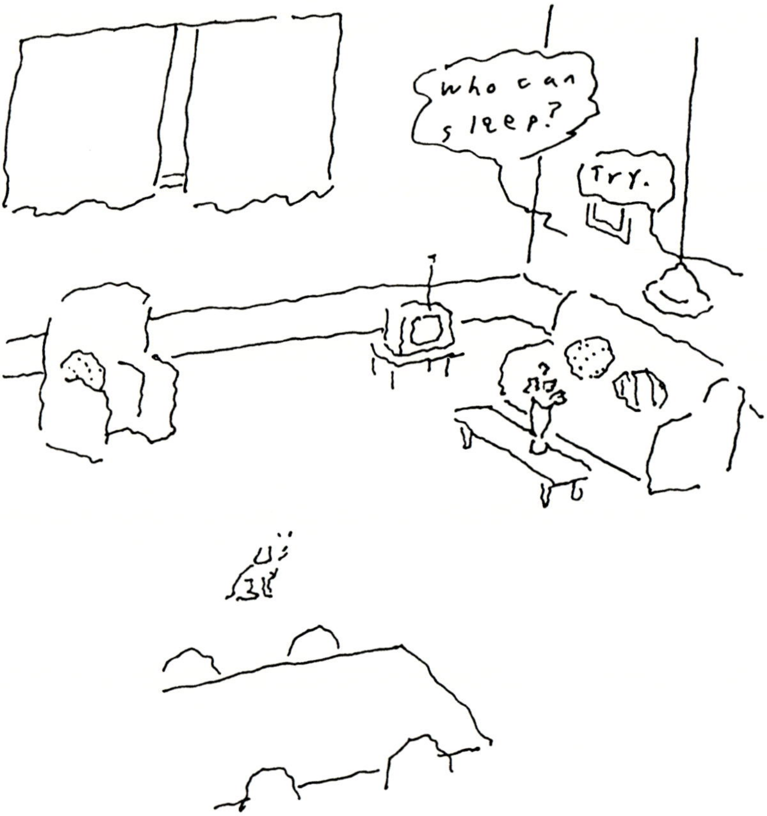
who can sleep?
Try.

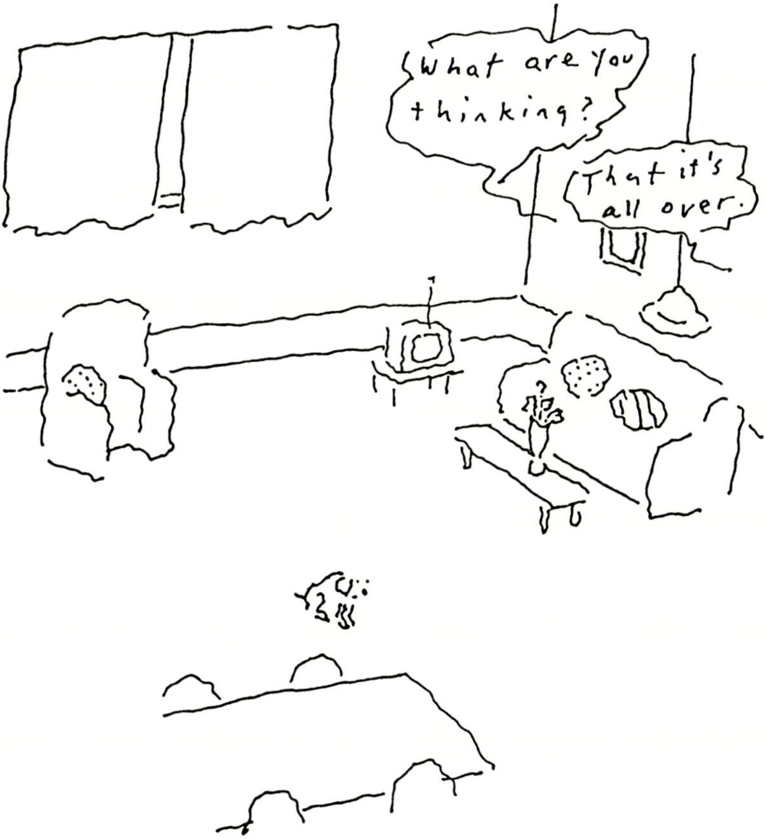
What are you thinking?
That it's all over.

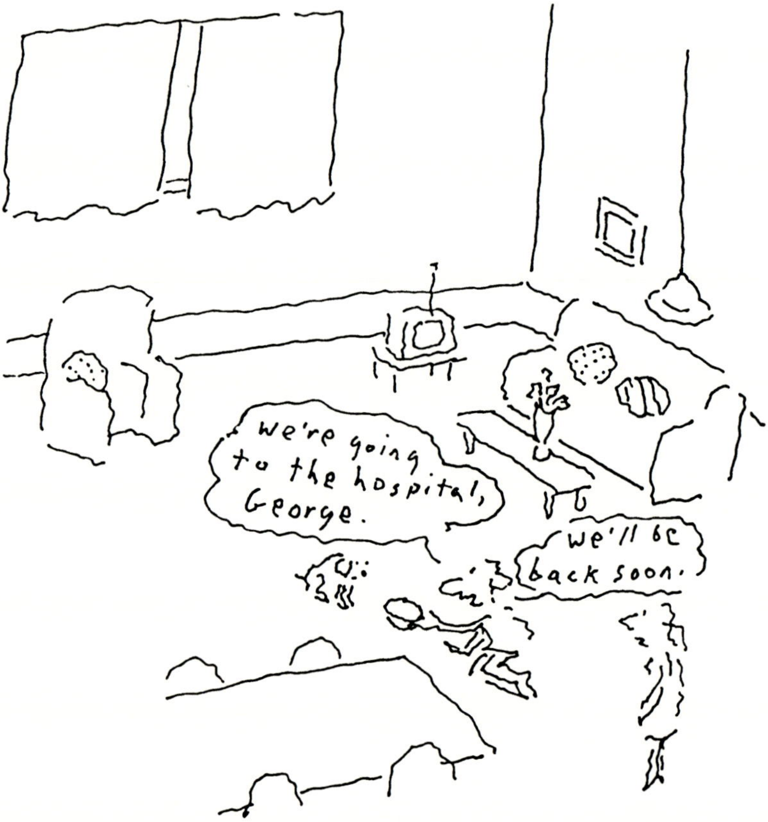
We're going
to the hospital,
George.
We'll be
back soon.

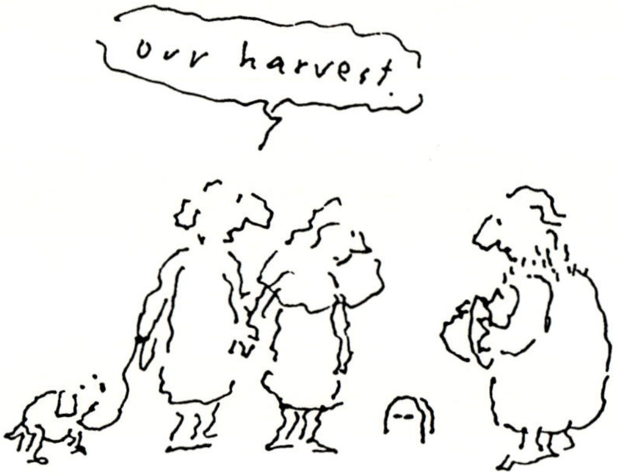
our harvest

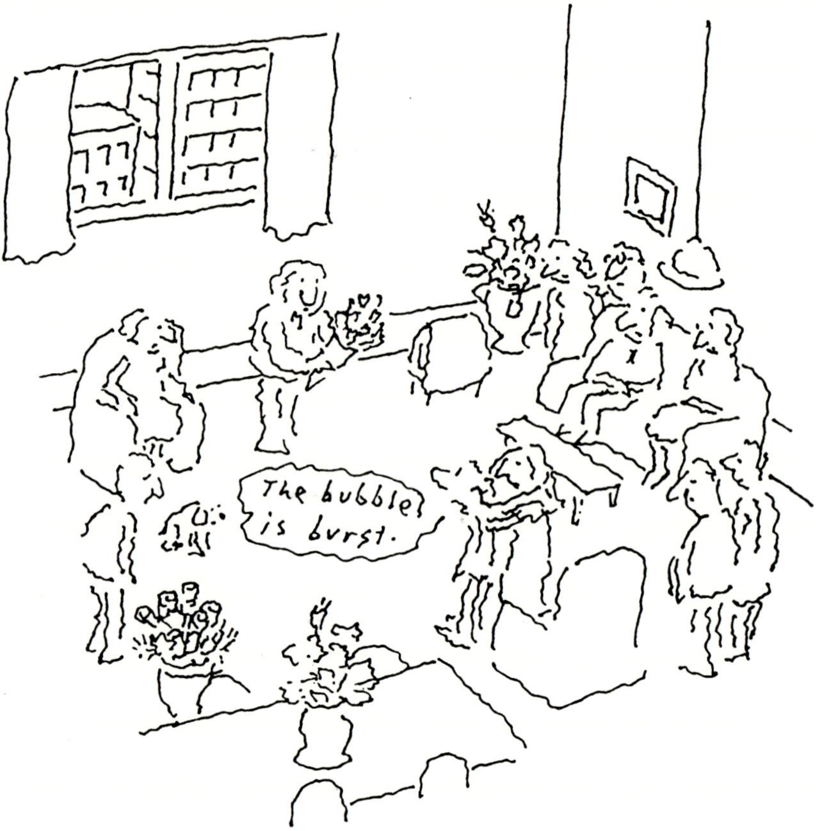
The bubble is burst.

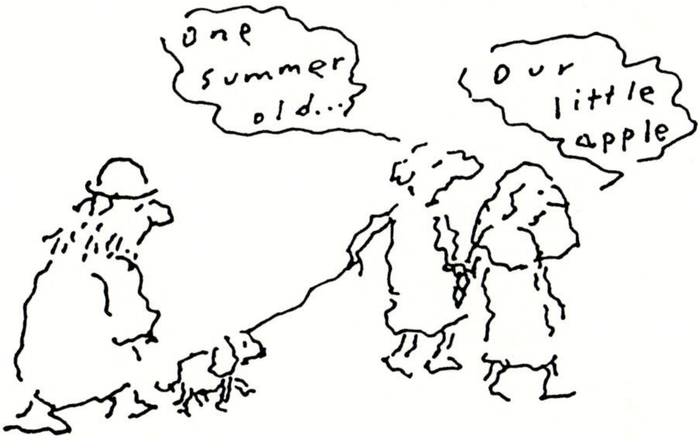
One summer old...
Our little apple

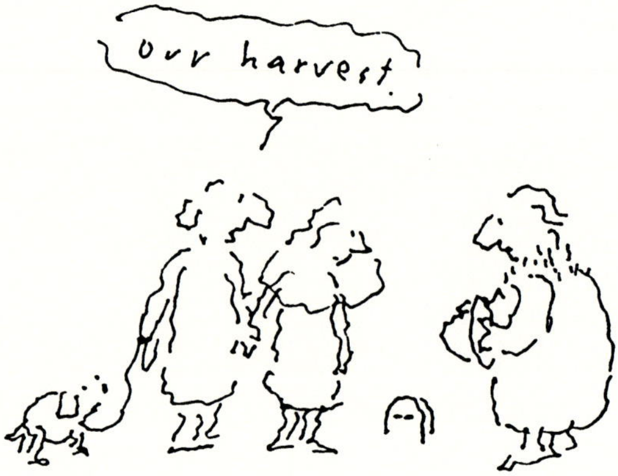
our harvest.

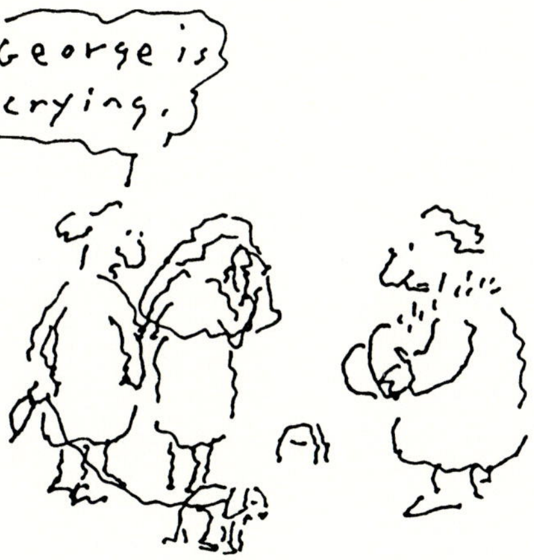
George is crying.

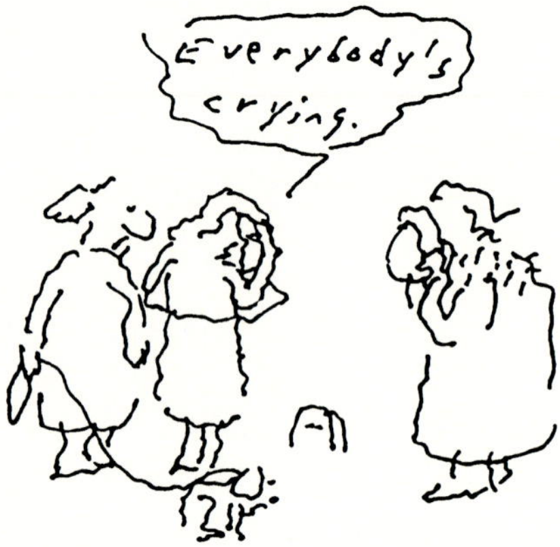
Everybody's crying.

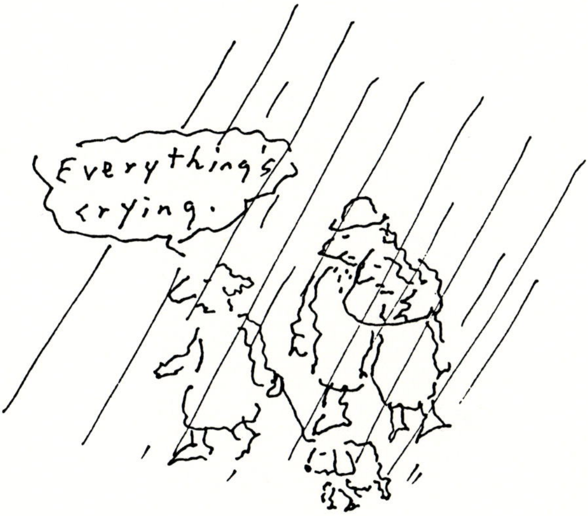
Everything's crying.

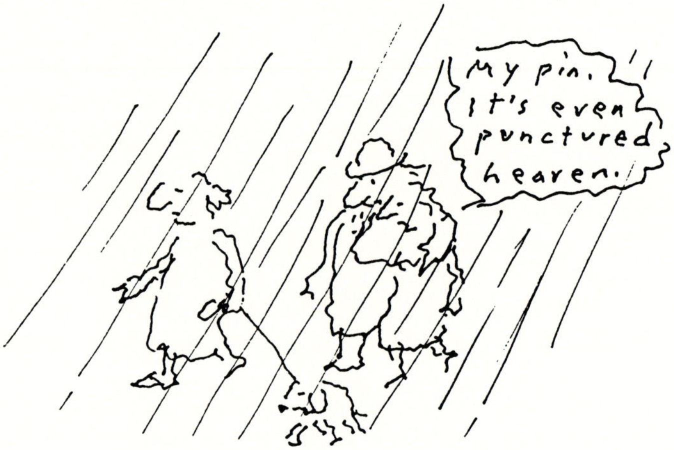
my pin. It's even punctured heaven.

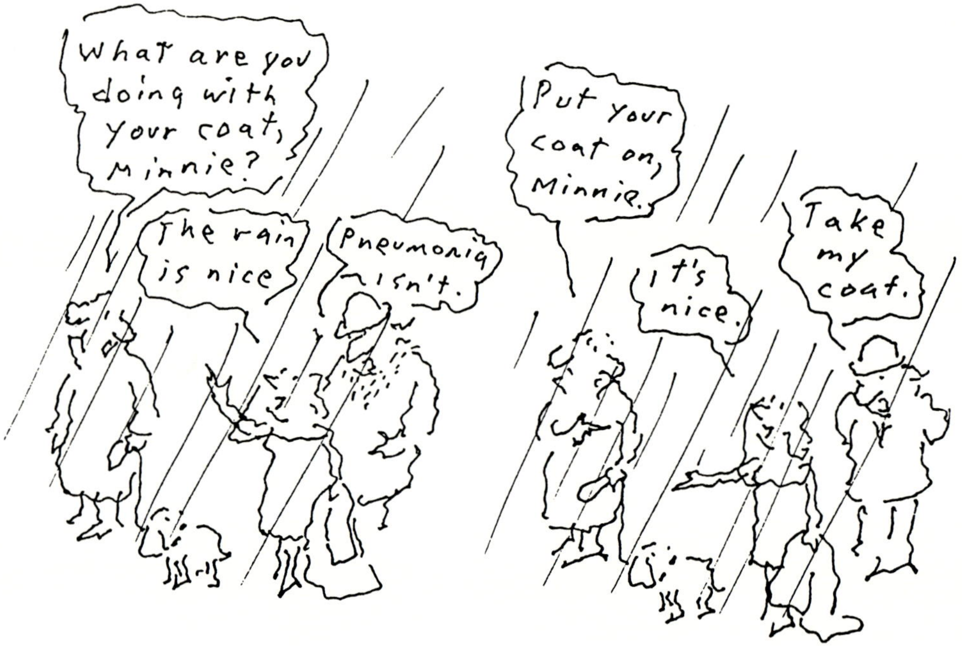
What are you doing with your coat, Minnie?
The rain is nice
Pneumonia isn't.
Put your coat on, Minnie.
It's nice.
Take my coat.

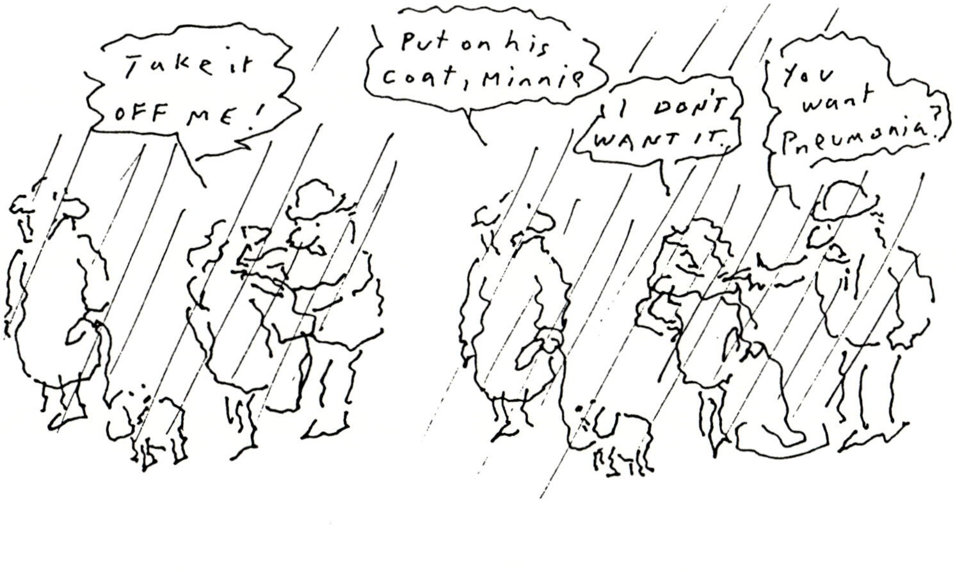
Take it OFF ME!
Put on his coat, Minnie
I DON'T WANT IT.
You want Pneumonia?

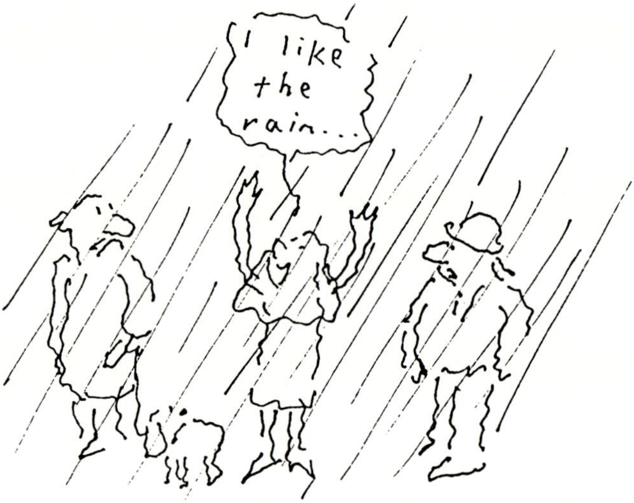
I like the rain...

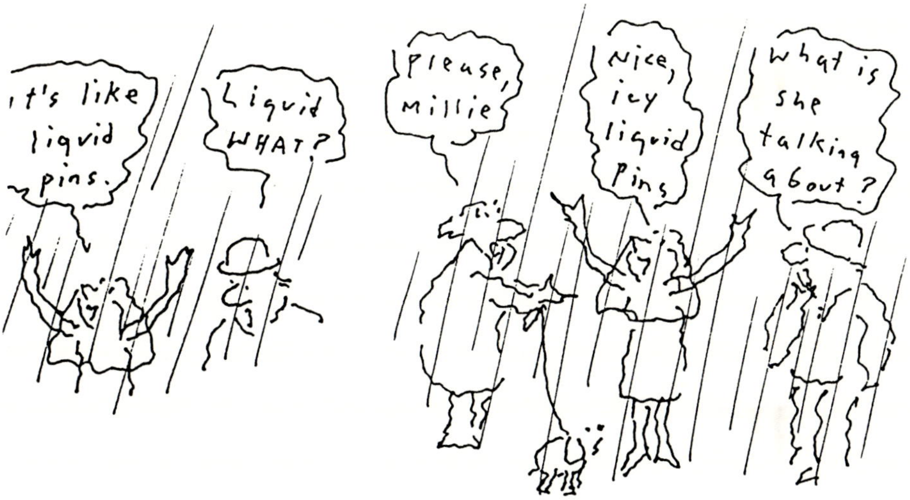
it's like liquid pins.
Liquid WHAT?
please, millie
Nice, icy liquid pins
what is she talking about?

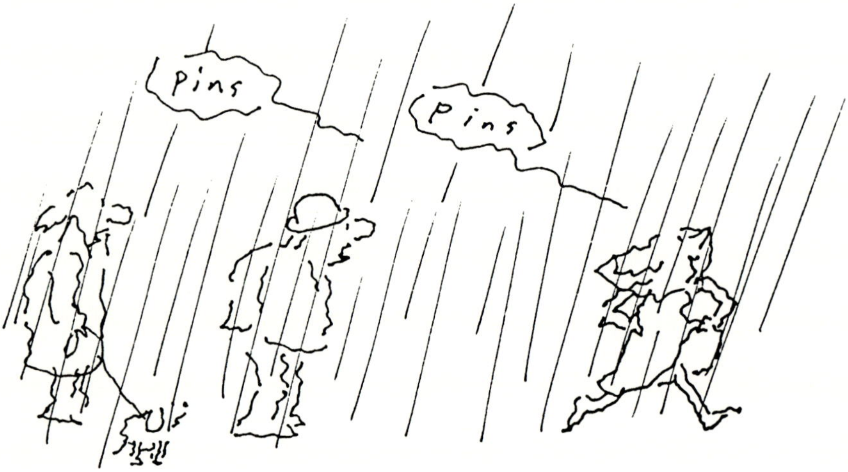
pins
pins

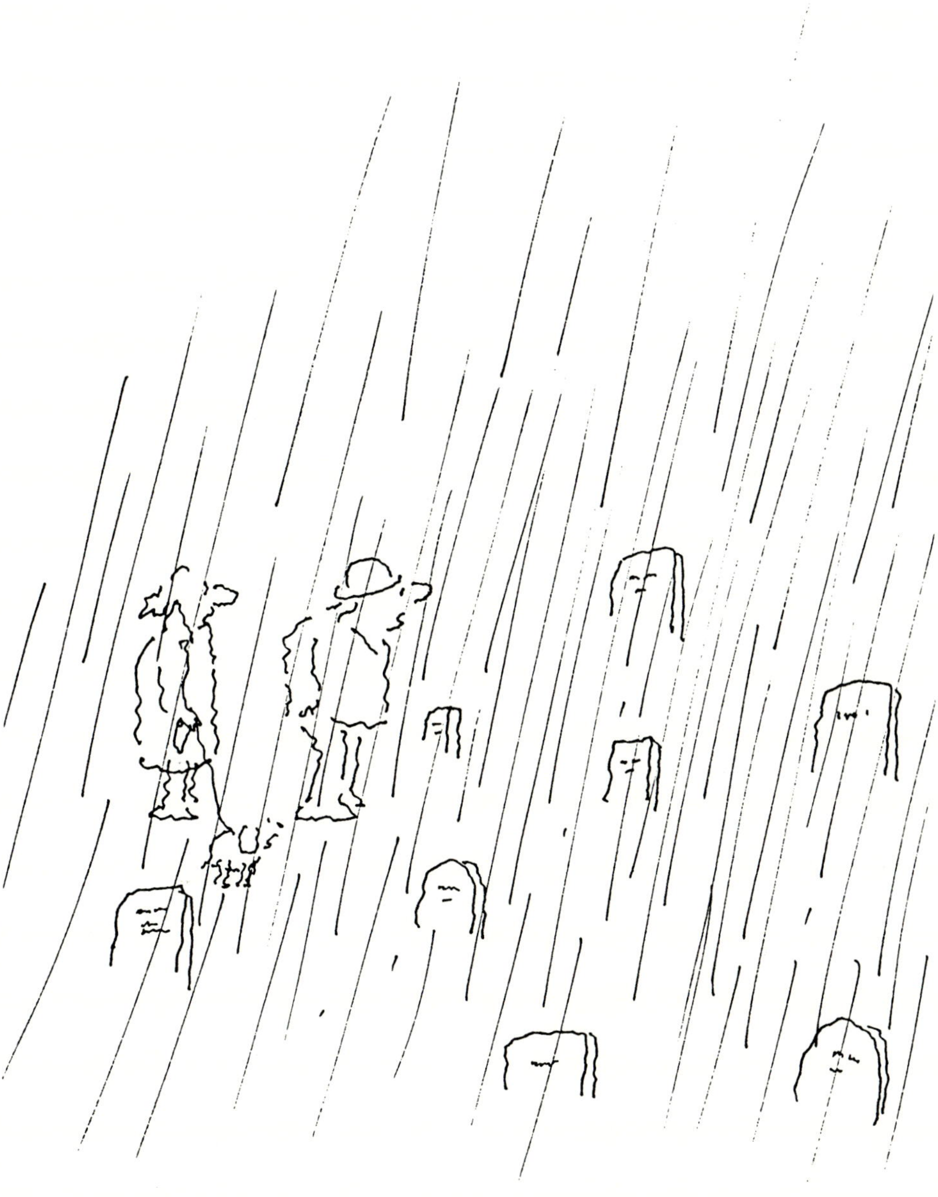

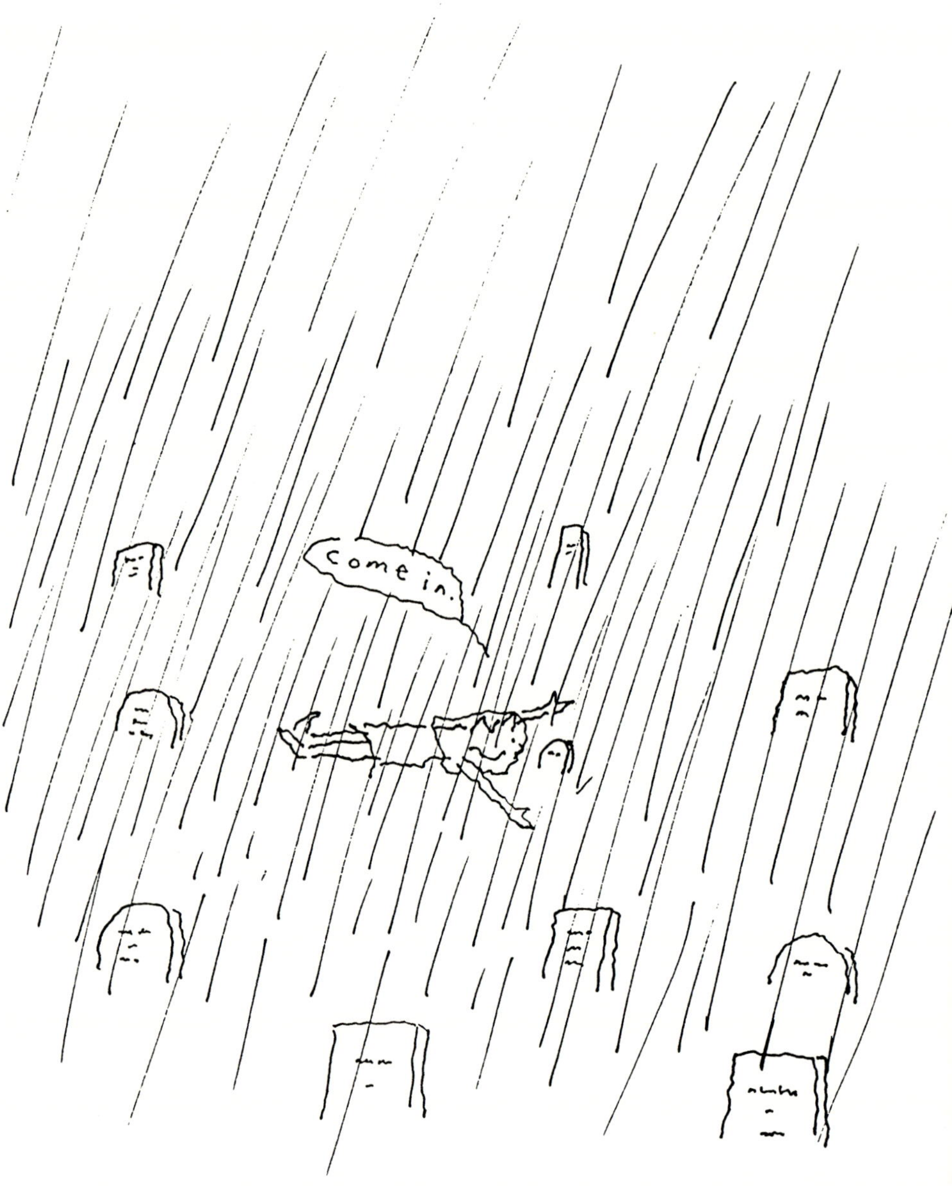
come in.

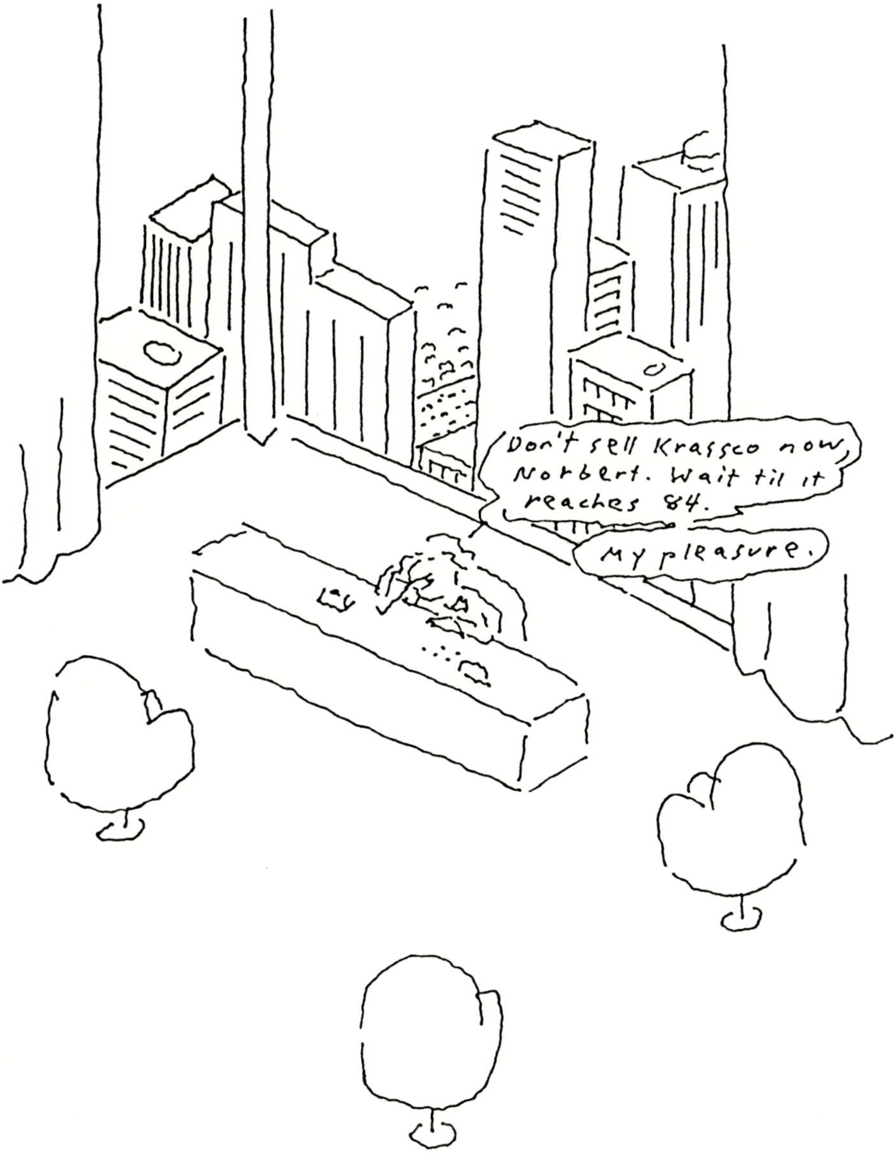
Don't sell Krassco now, Norbert. Wait til it reaches 84.
My pleasure.

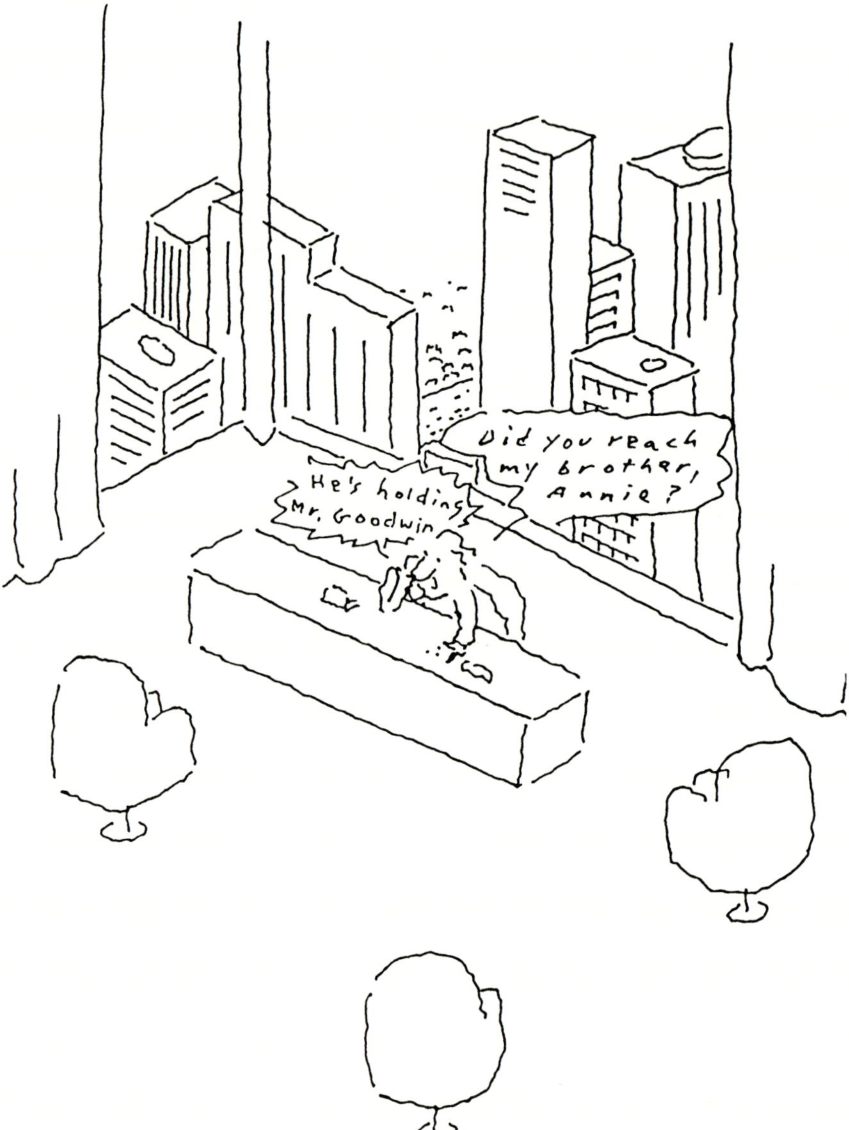

He's holding Mr. Goodwin
Did you reach my brother, Annie?

Hello, Arnold,
it's Wenty.

I transferred Alex's
stocks to your account.
And Minnie's too,
of course.

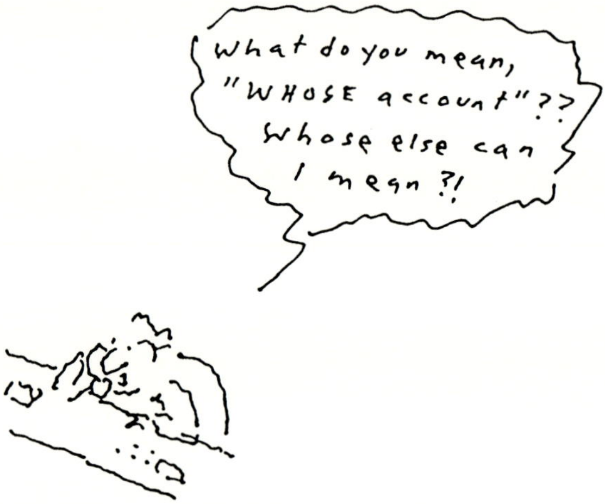
What do you mean, "WHOSE account"?? Whose else can I mean?!

What are you saying, "UNFEELING"?! I'm a stockbroker not a RABBI!

Look, Arnold, I'll be over after work. I think we have to have a little talk.

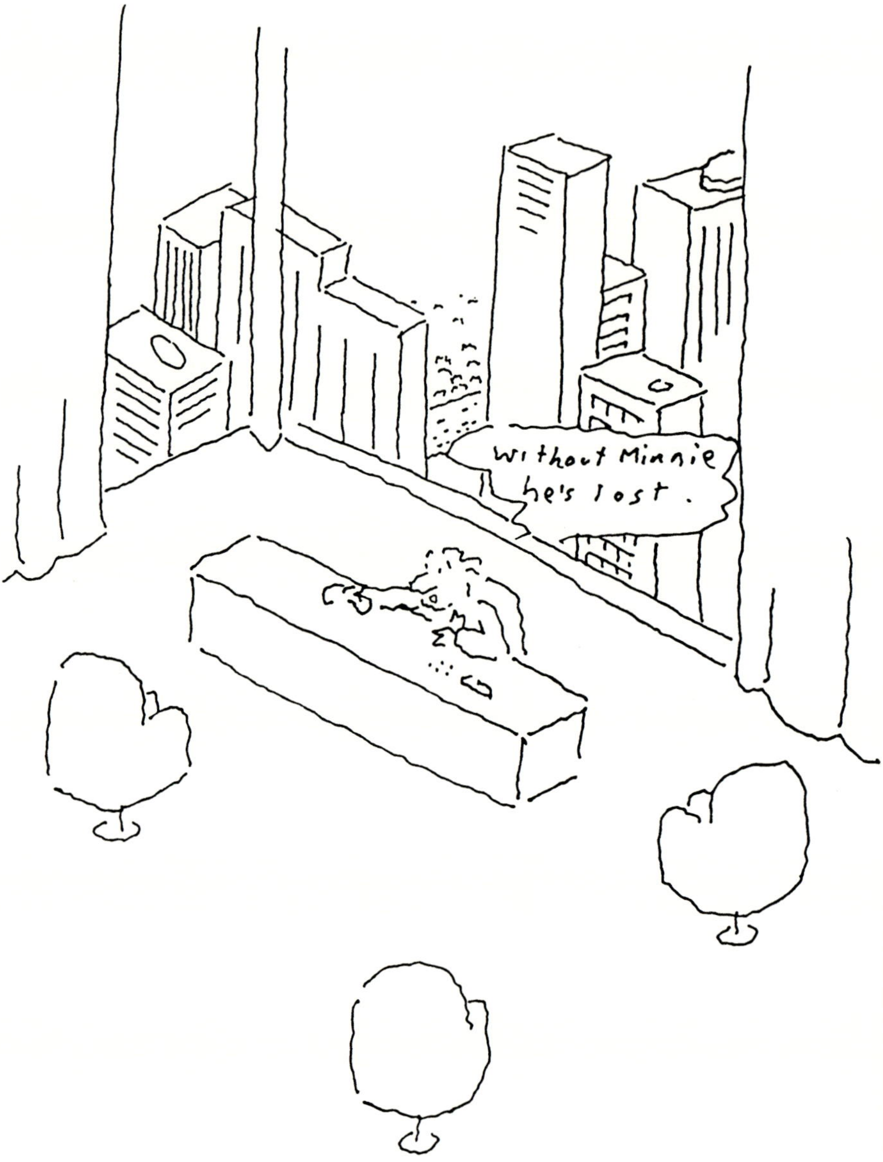
without Minnie
he's lost.

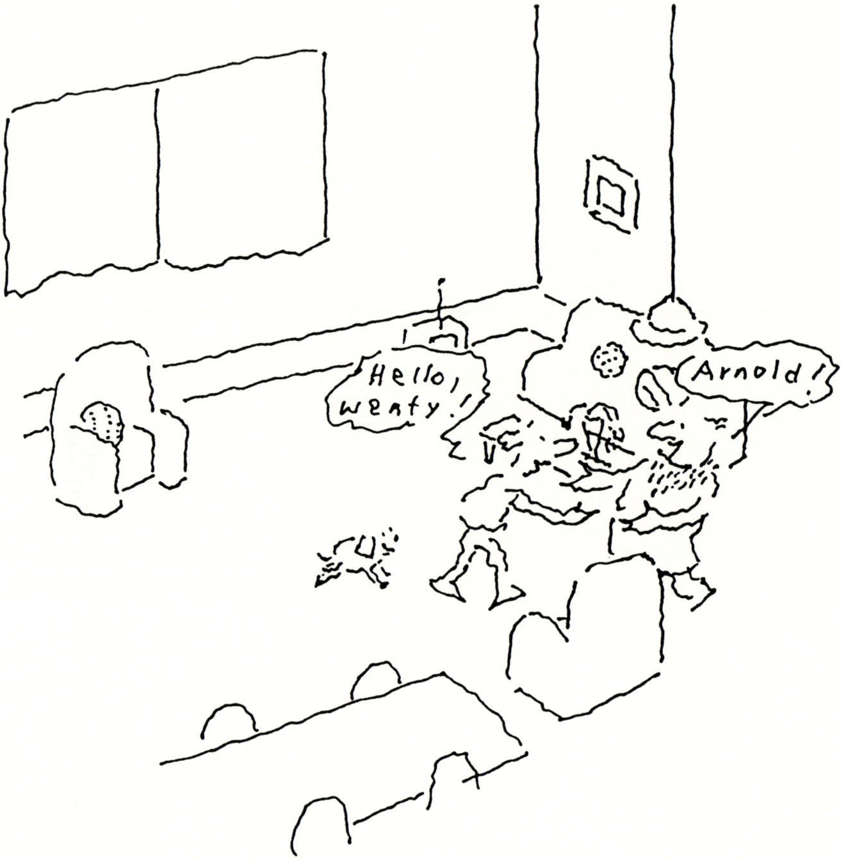
Hello, wenty!
Arnold!

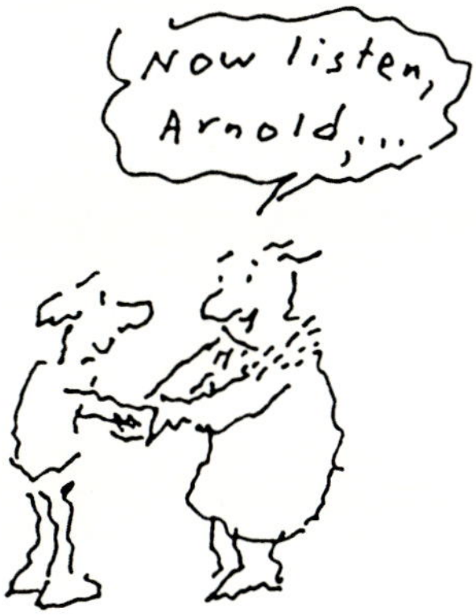
Now listen, Arnold,...

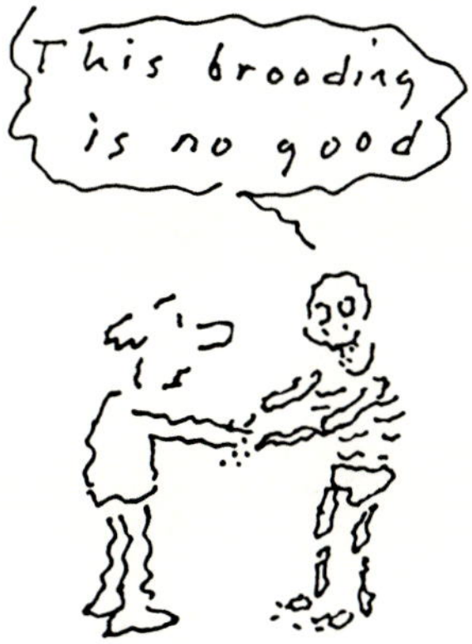
This brooding is no good

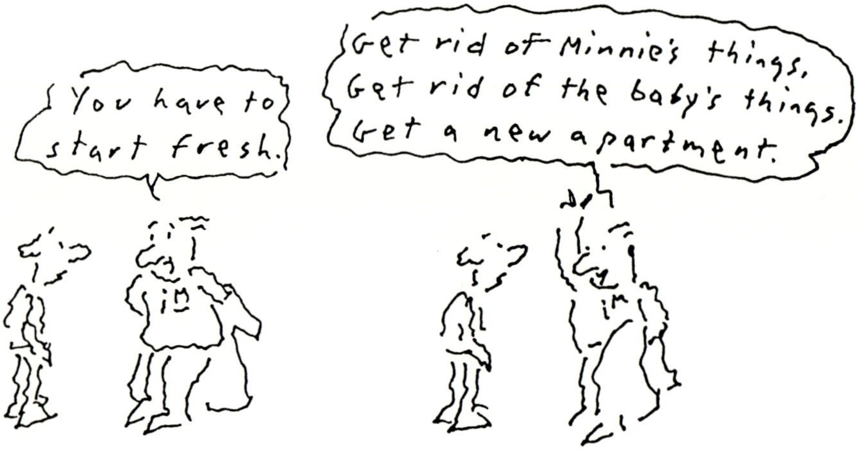

You have to start fresh.
Get rid of Minnie's things. Get rid of the baby's things. Get a new apartment.

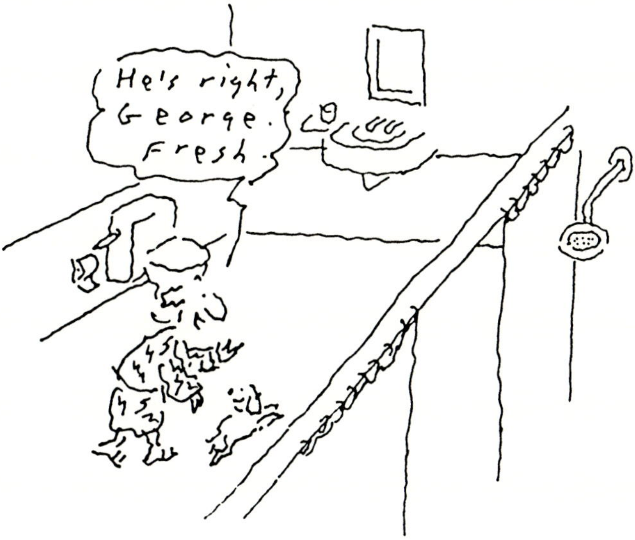
He's right, George. Fresh.

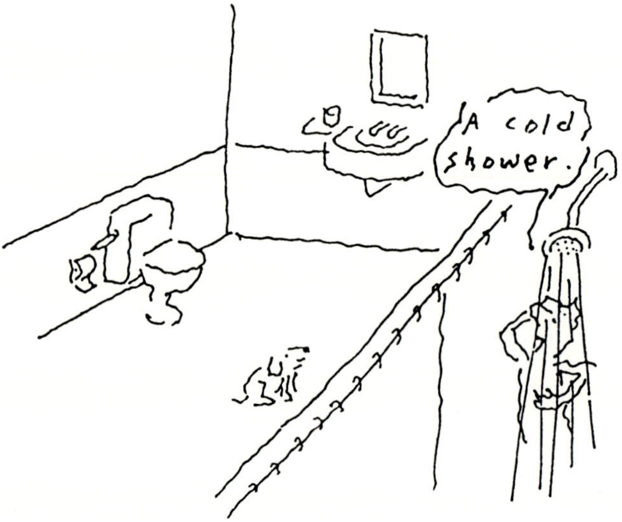
A cold shower.

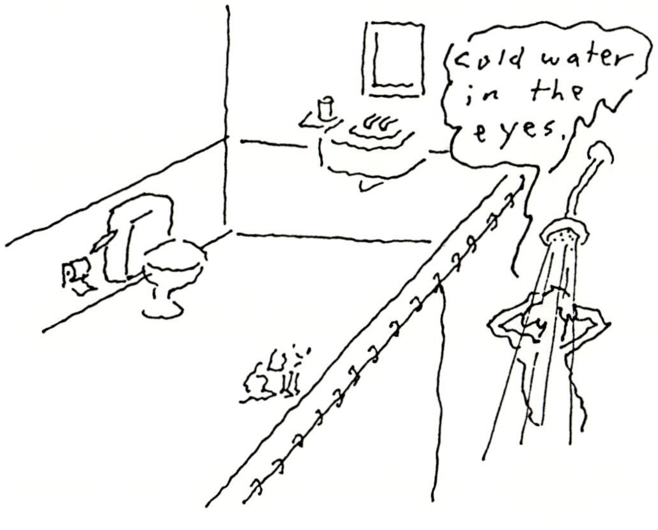
cold water in the eyes,

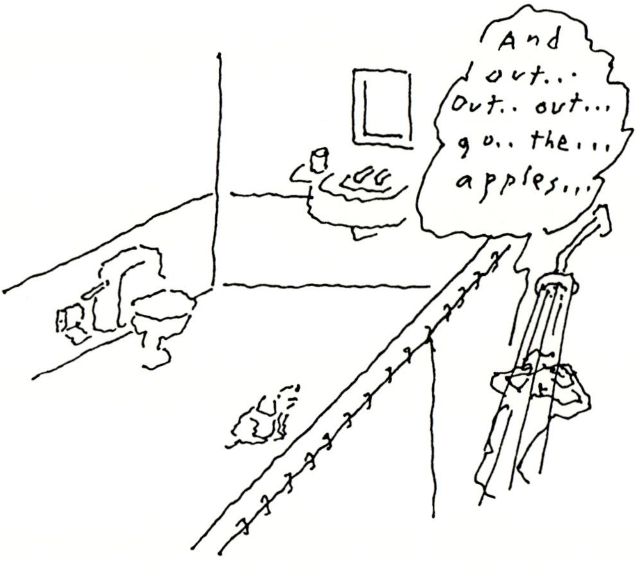
And out.. Out.. out... go.. the... apples...

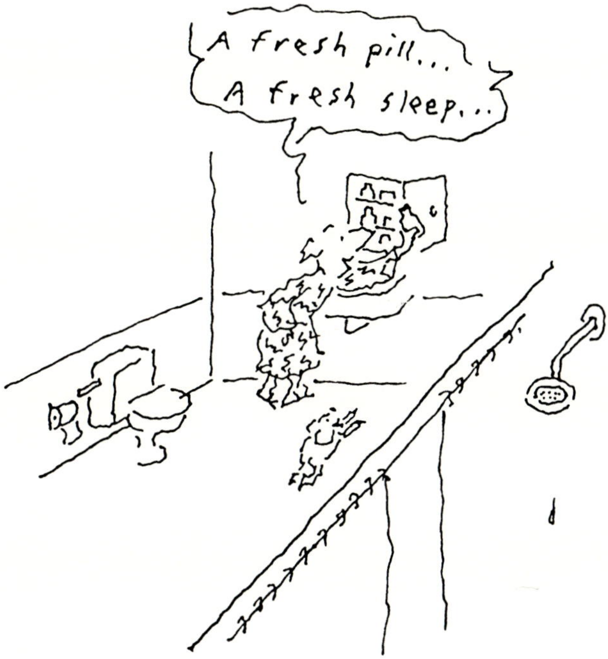
A fresh pill...
A fresh sleep...

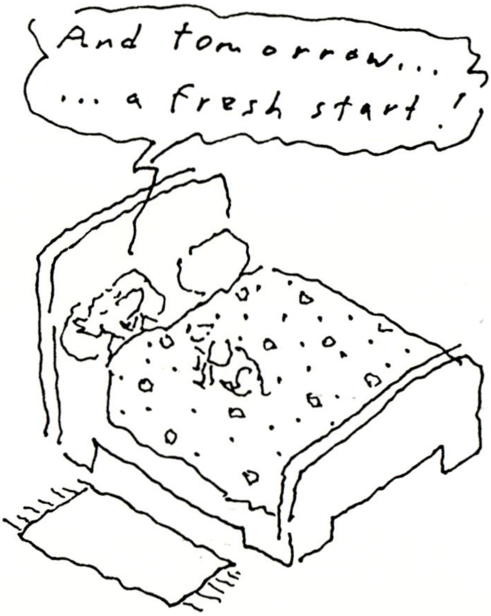
And tomorrow...
... a fresh start!

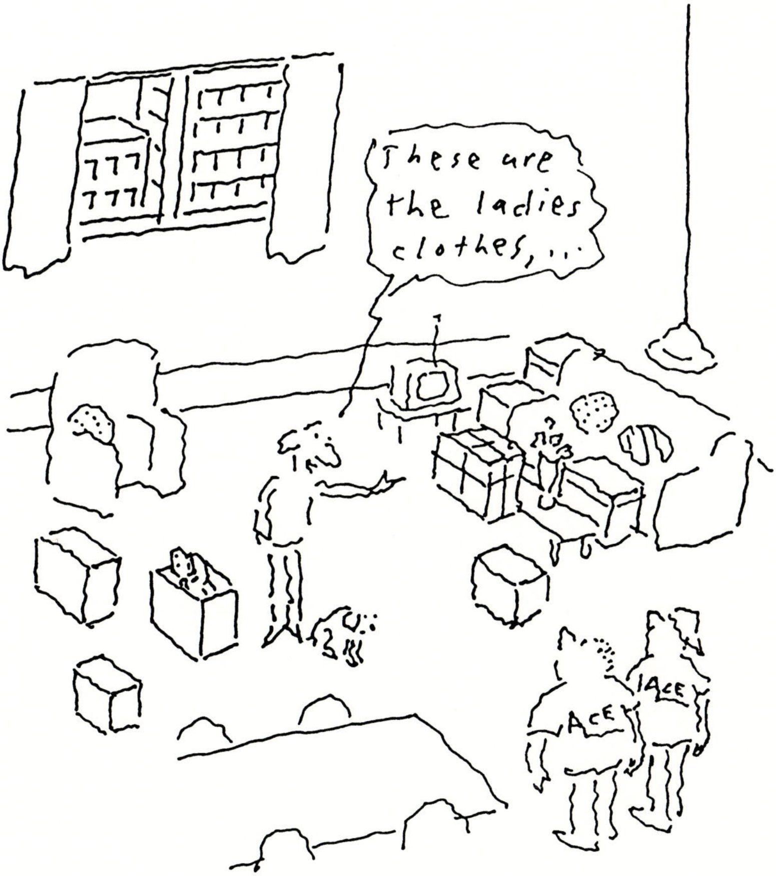
These are the ladies clothes, ...
ACE
ACE

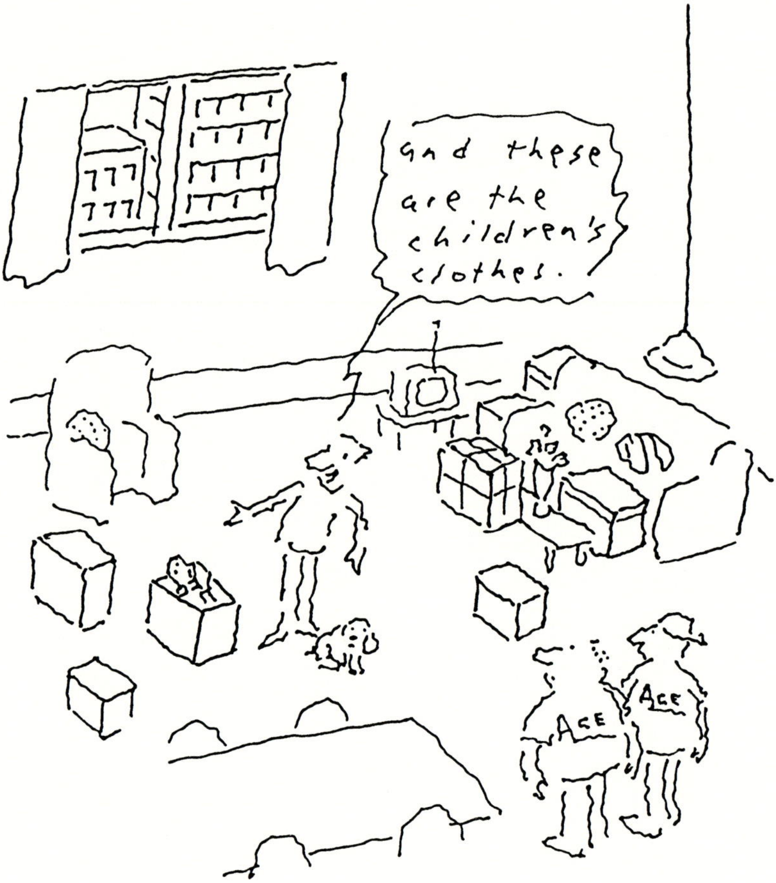
and these are the children's clothes.
ACE
ACE

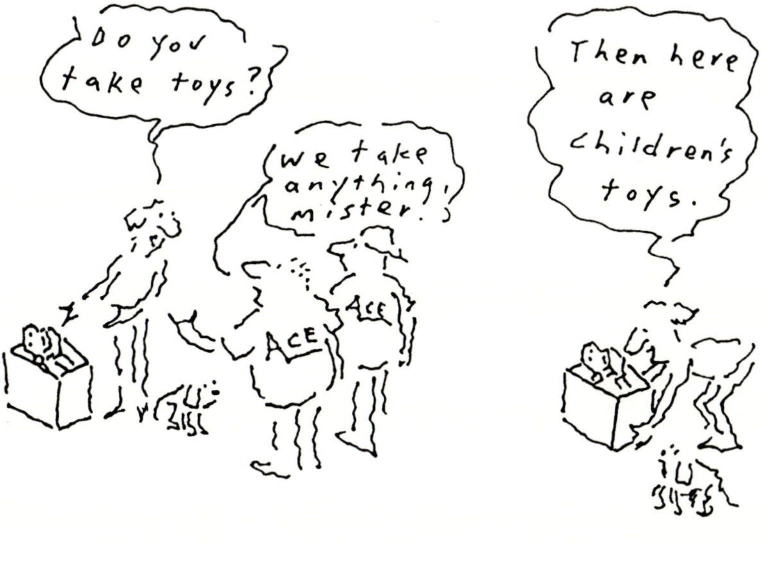
Do you take toys?
We take anything, mister!
Then here are children's toys.

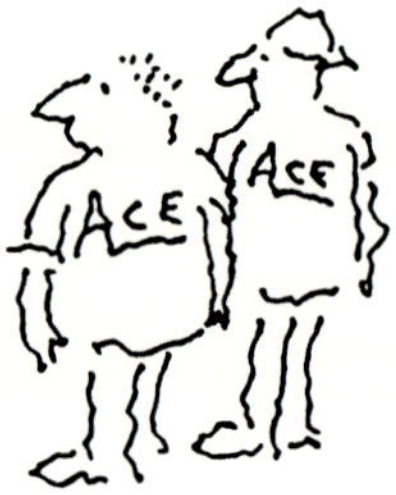
ACE
ACE

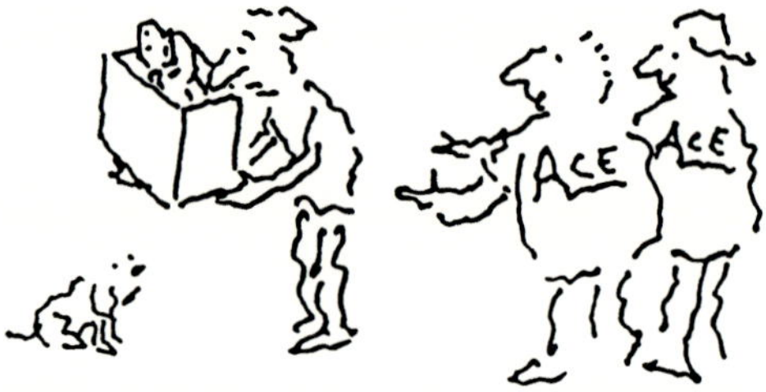
ACE
ACE

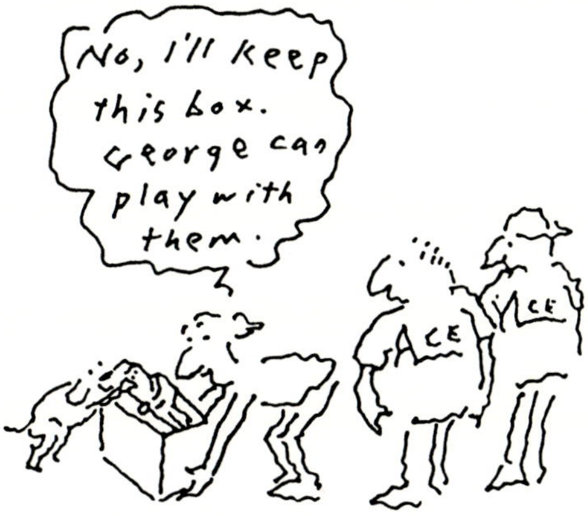
No, I'll keep this box. George can play with them.

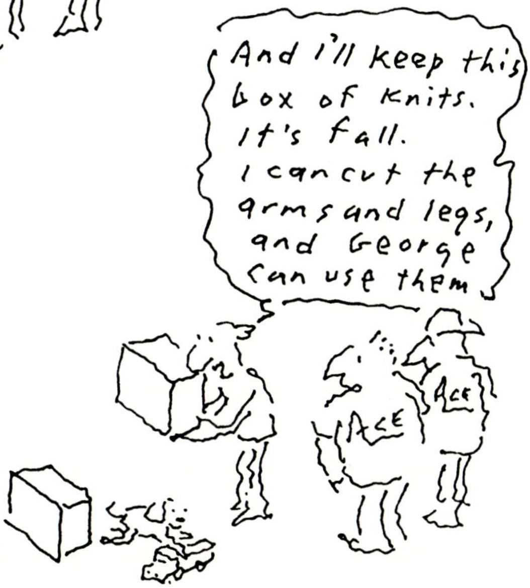
And I'll keep this box of knits. It's fall. I can cut the arms and legs, and George can use them.

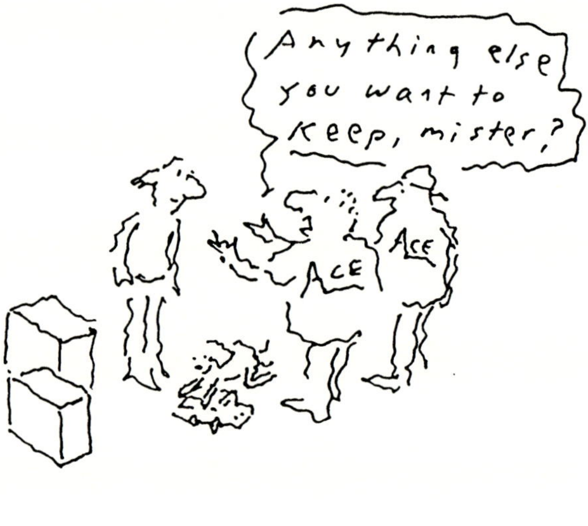
Anything else you want to keep, mister?
ACE
ACE

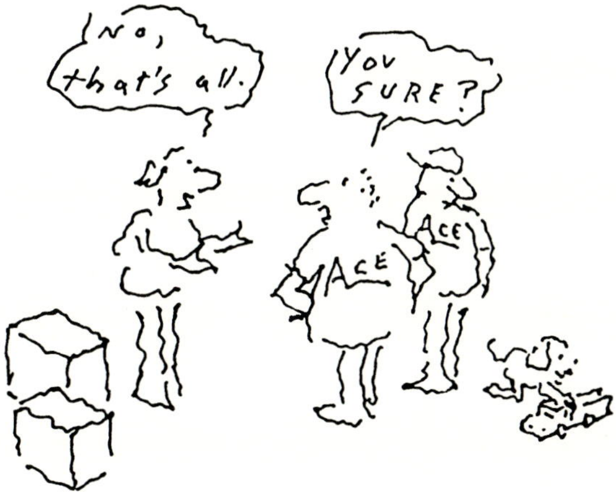
No, that's all.
You SURE?
ACE
ACE

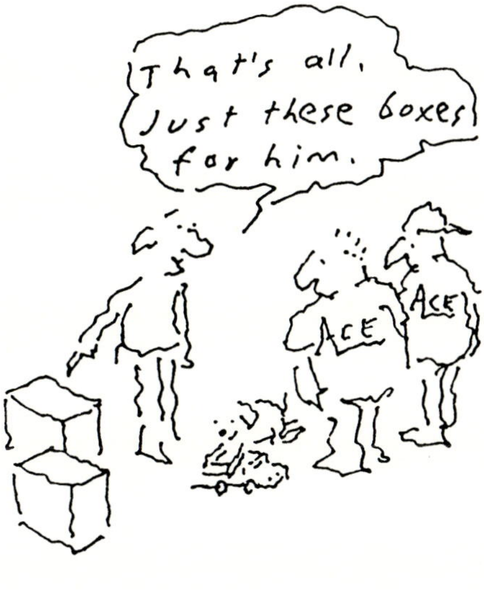
That's all. Just these boxes for him.
ACE
ACE

ACE
ACE

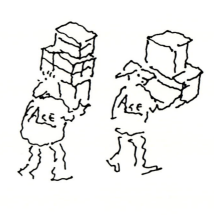

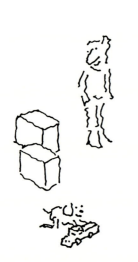

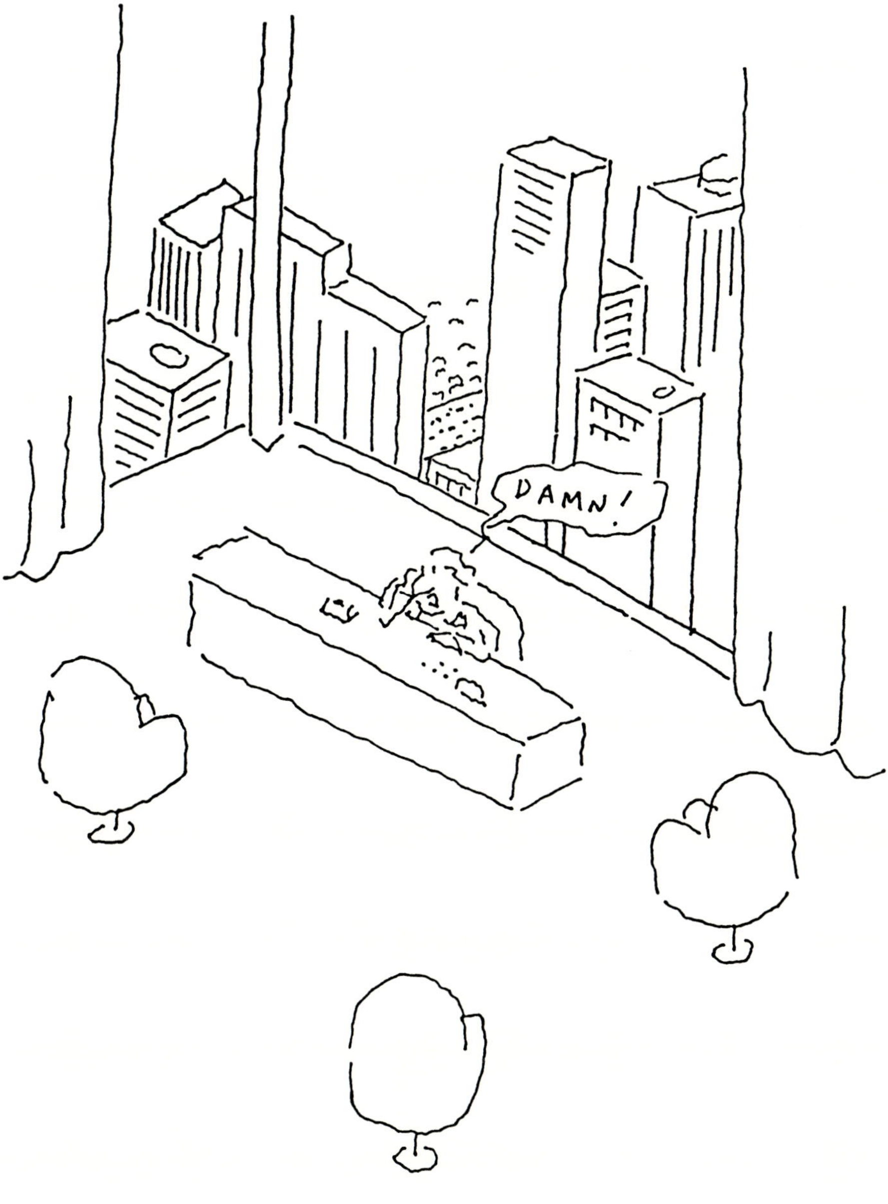
DAMN!

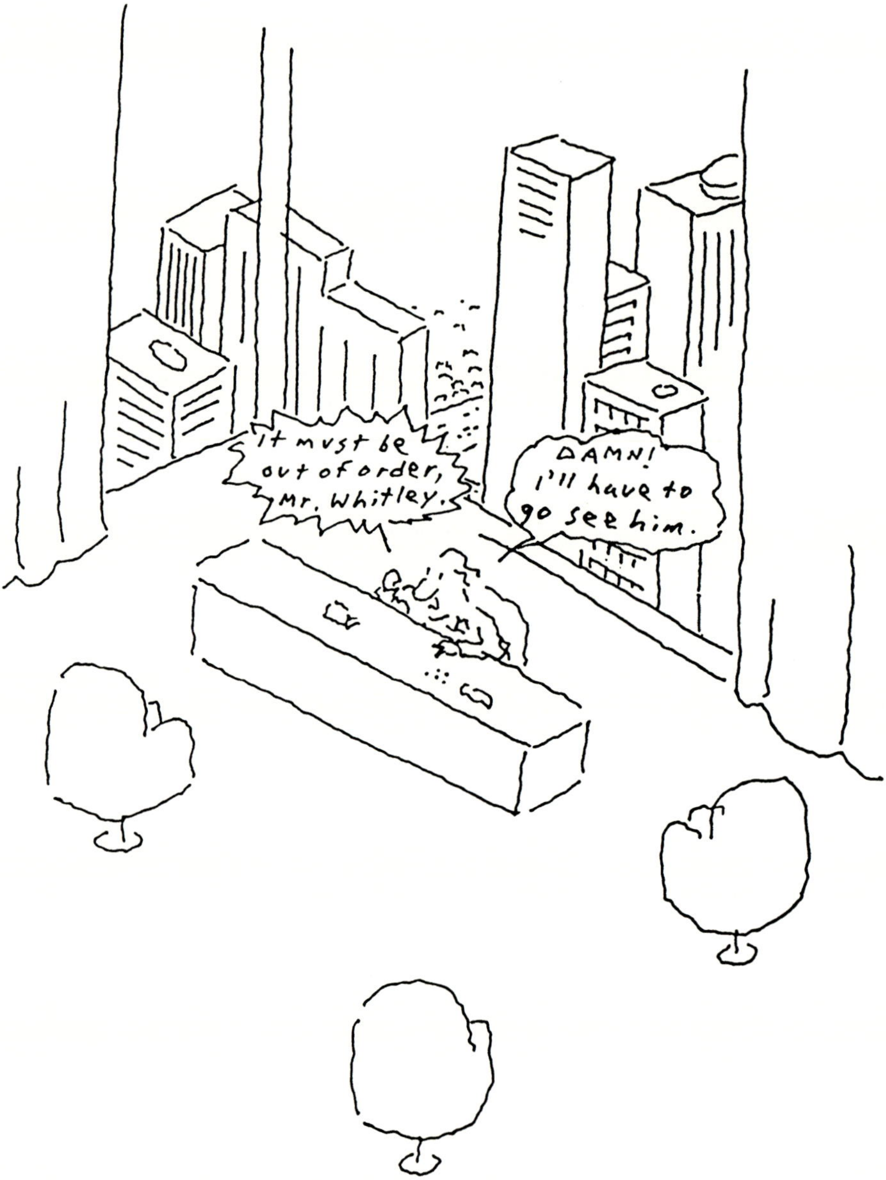
It must be out of order, Mr. Whitley.
DAMN! I'll have to go see him.

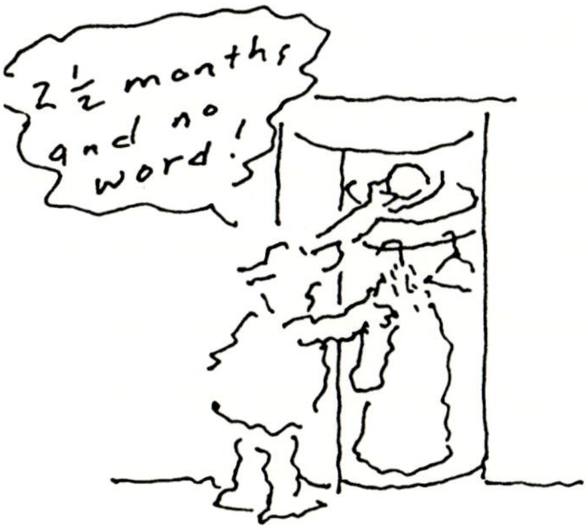
2½ months and no word!

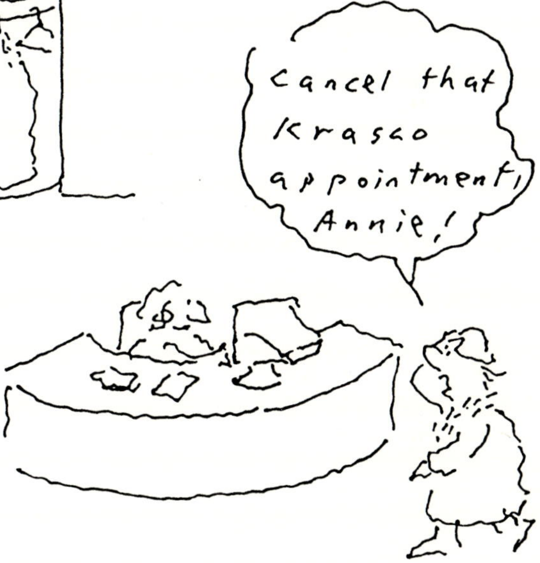
Cancel that Krasco appointment, Annie!

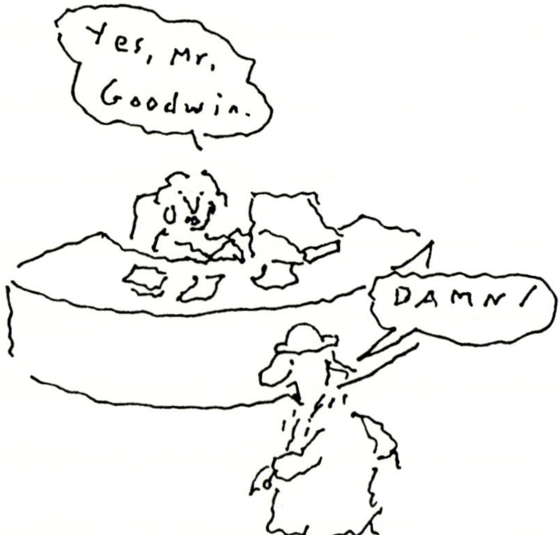
Yes, Mr.
Goodwin.
DAMN!

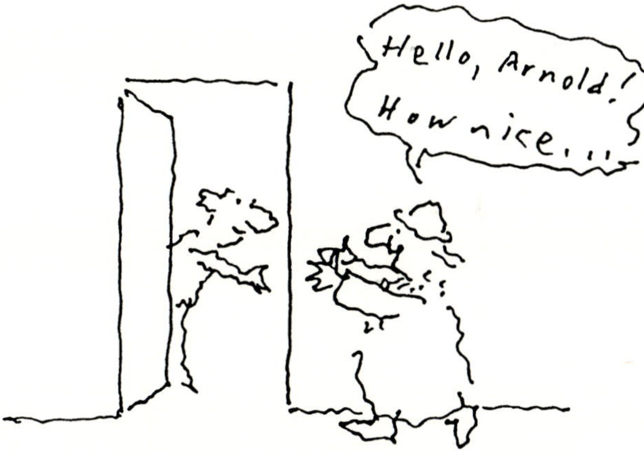
Hello, Arnold! How nice...

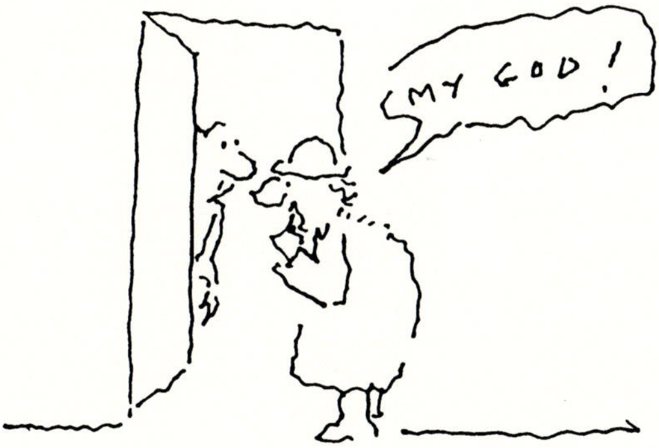
MY GOD!

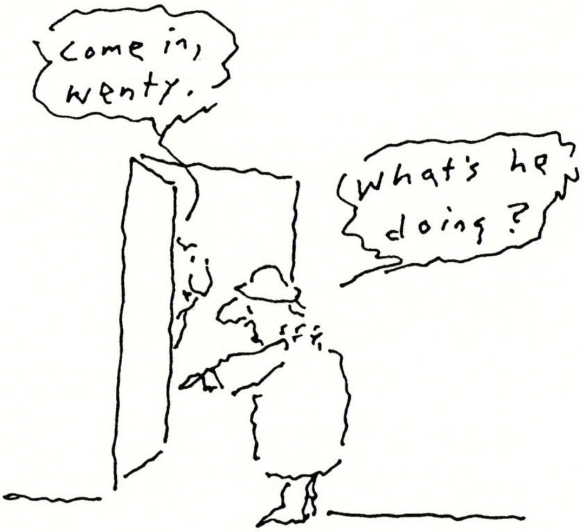
come in,
wenty.
what's he
doing?

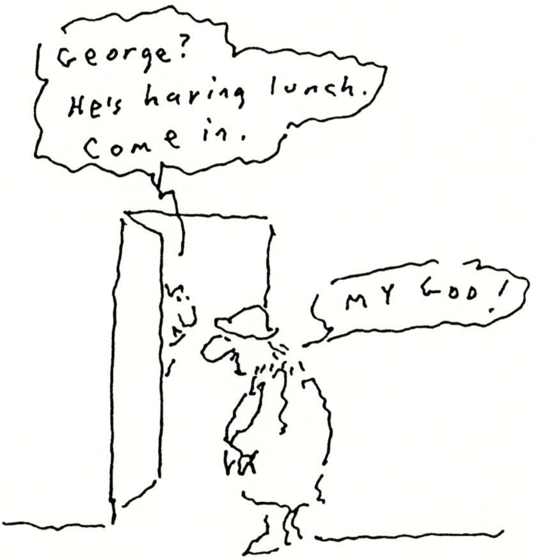
George?
He's having lunch.
Come in.
MY GOD!

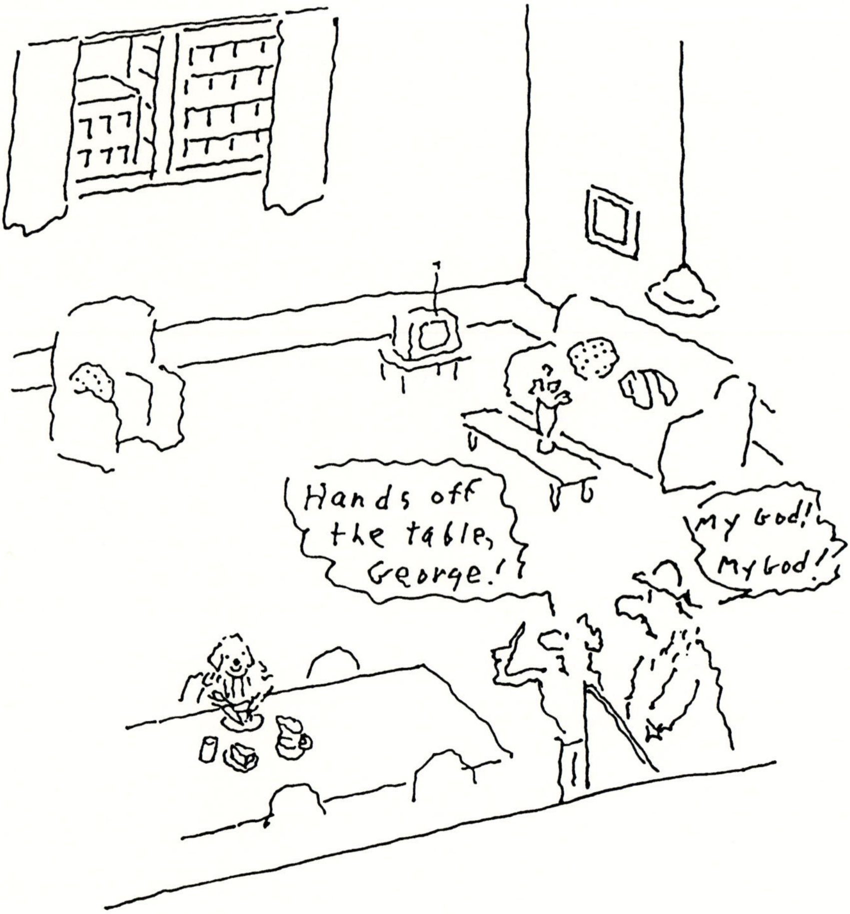
Hands off the table, George!
My God! My God!

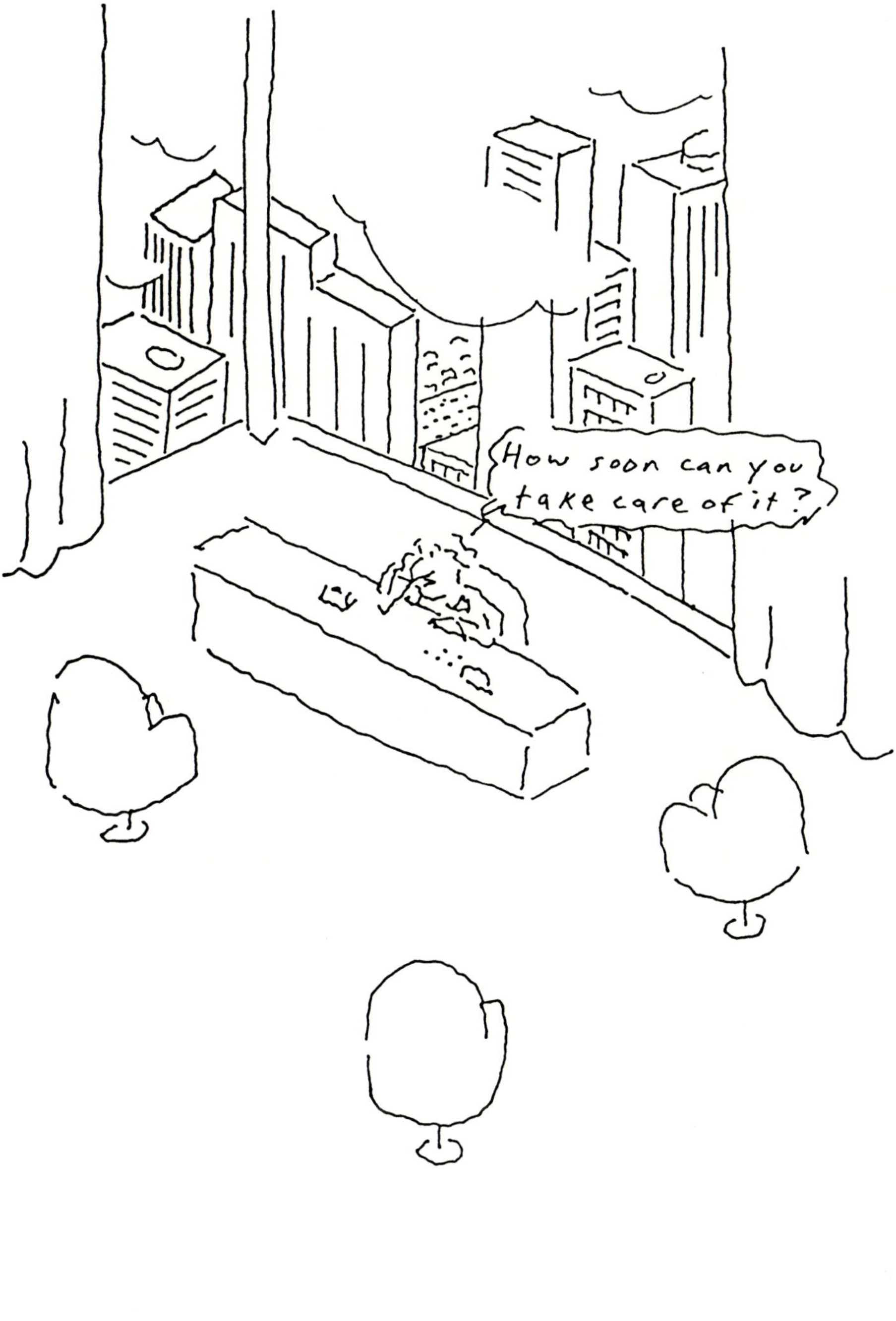
How soon can you take care of it?

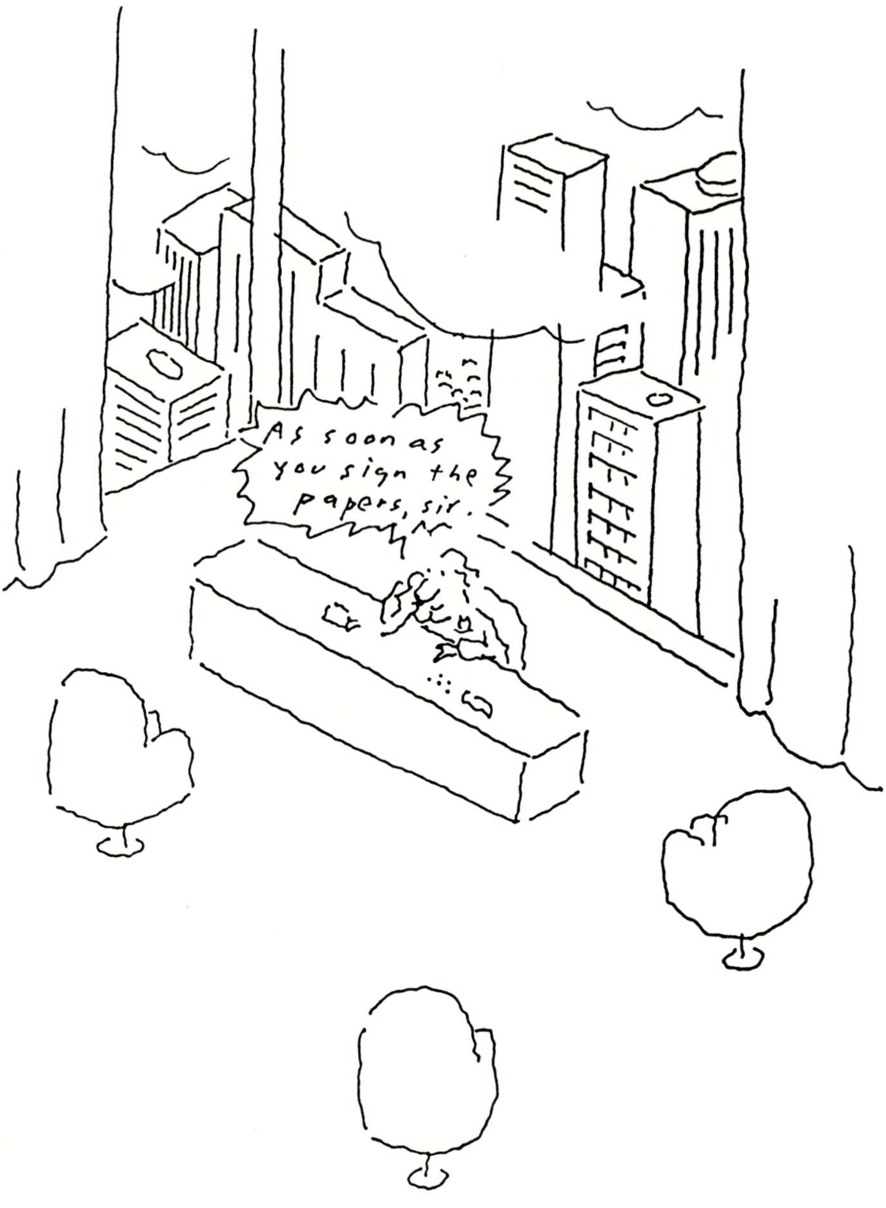
As soon as you sign the papers, sir.

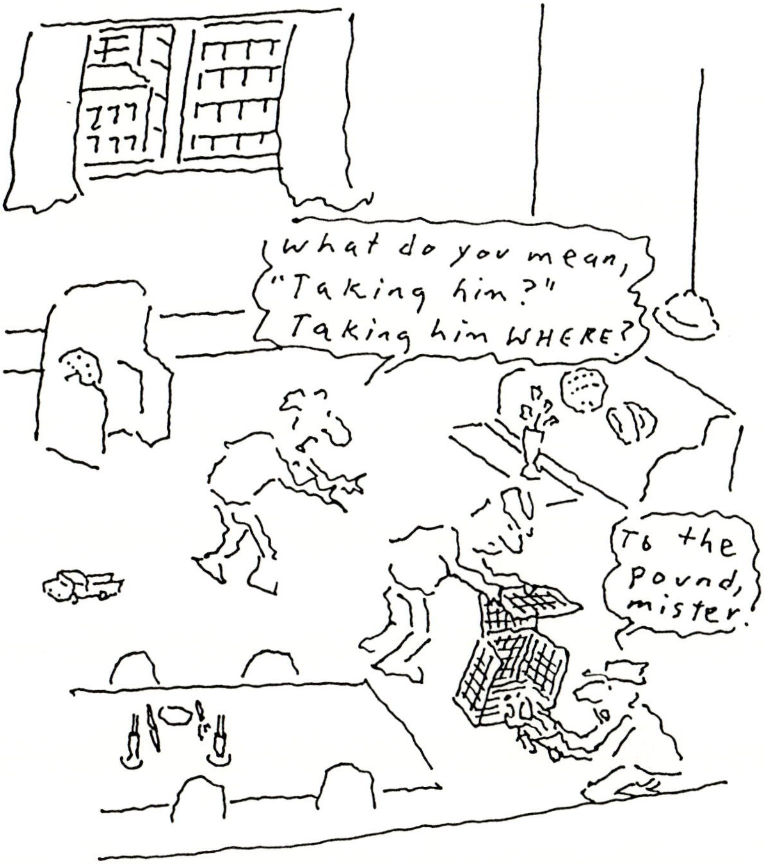
What do you mean, "Taking him?" Taking him WHERE?
To the pound, mister.

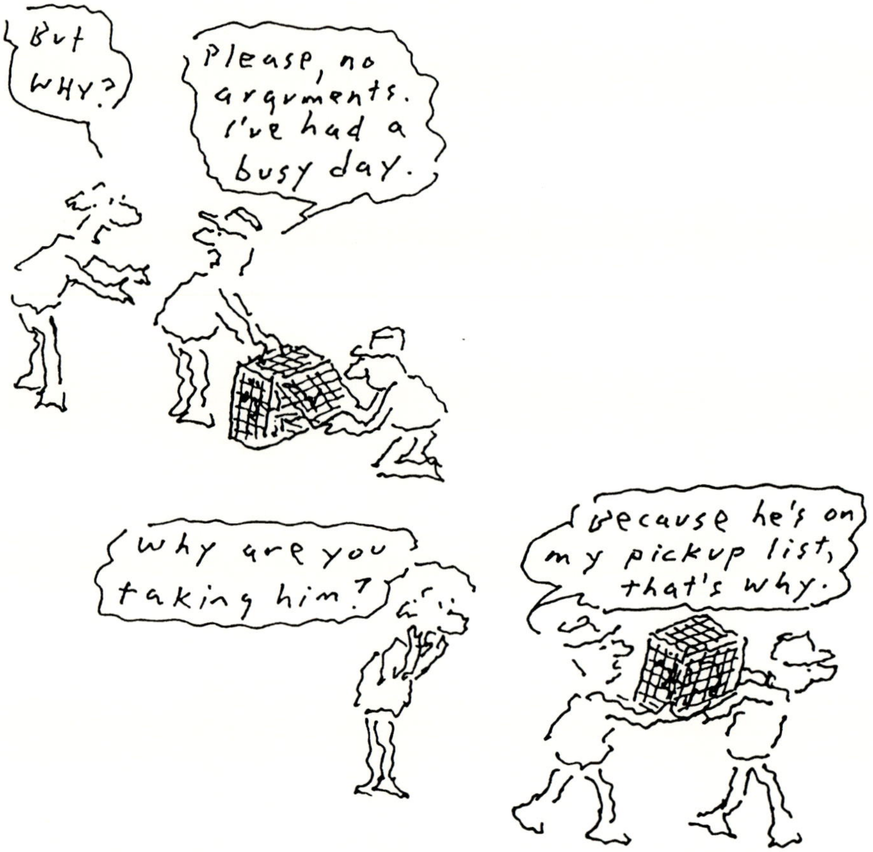
But WHY?
Please, no arguments. I've had a busy day.
Why are you taking him?
Because he's on my pickup list, that's why.

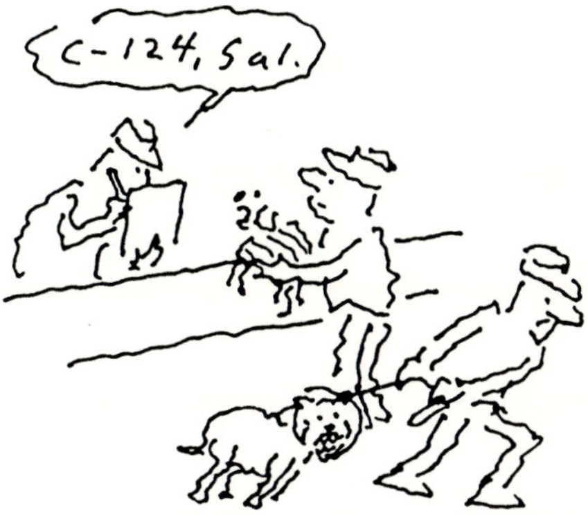
C-124, Sal.

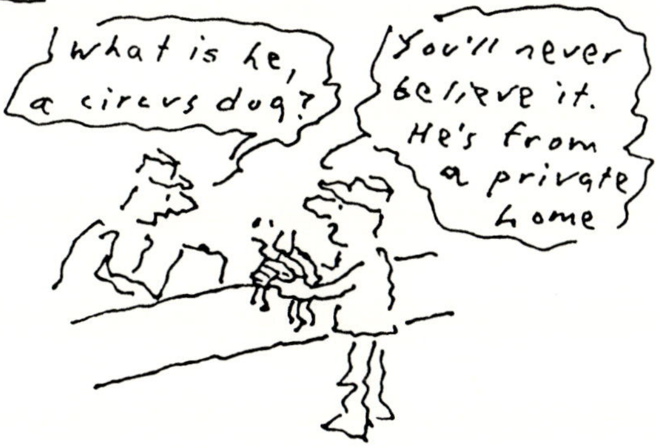
What is he, a circus dog?
You'll never believe it. He's from a private home

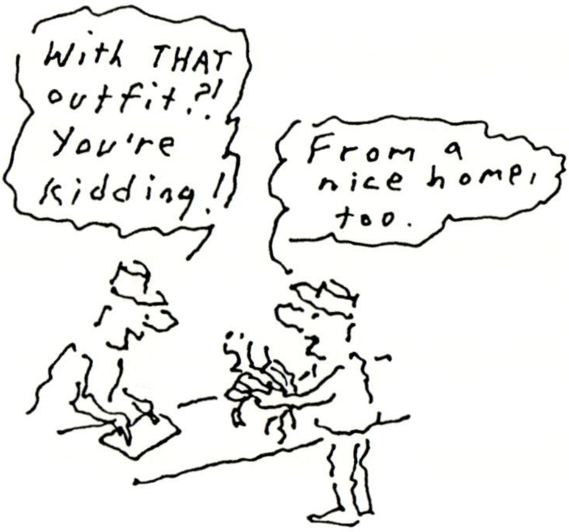
With THAT outfit?! You're kidding!
From a nice home, too.

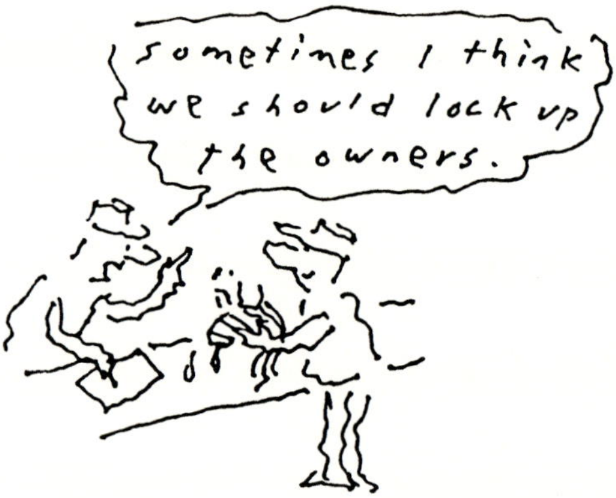
sometimes I think we should lock up the owners.

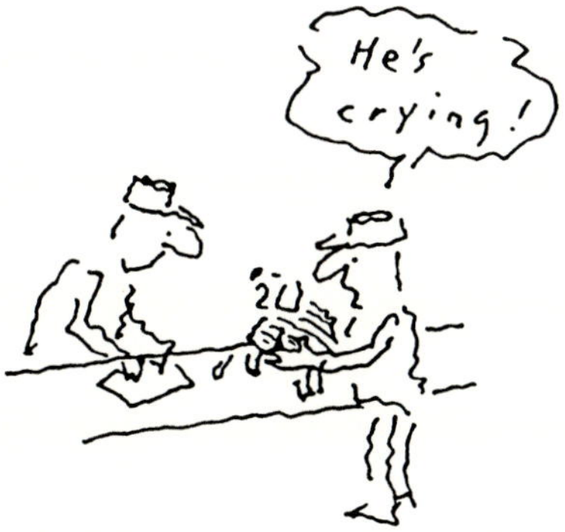
He's crying!

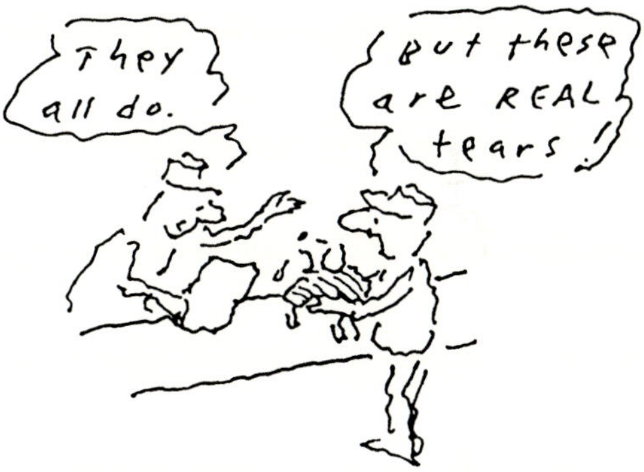
They all do.
But these are REAL tears!

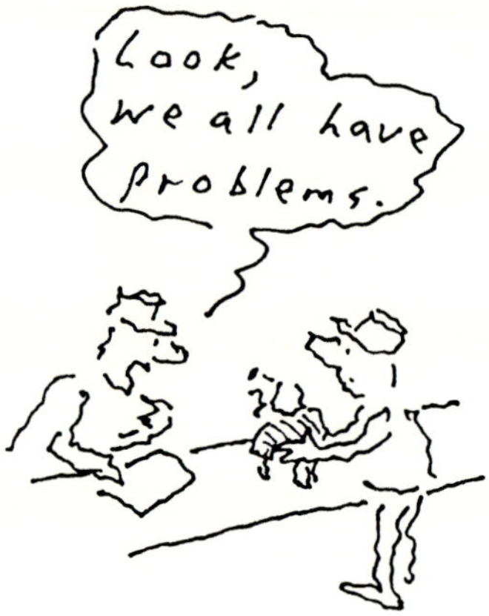
Look, we all have problems.

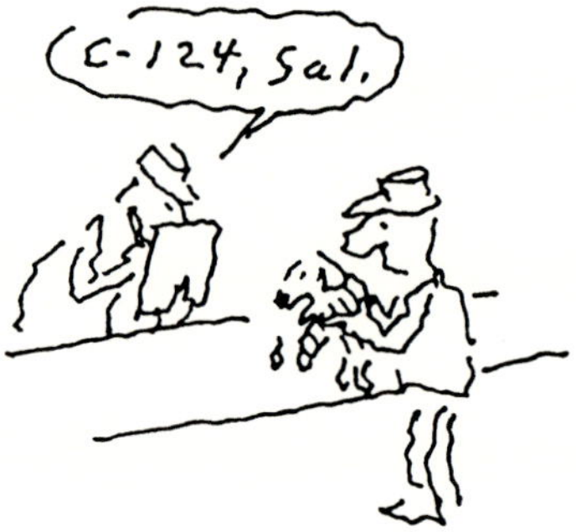
C-124, Sal.

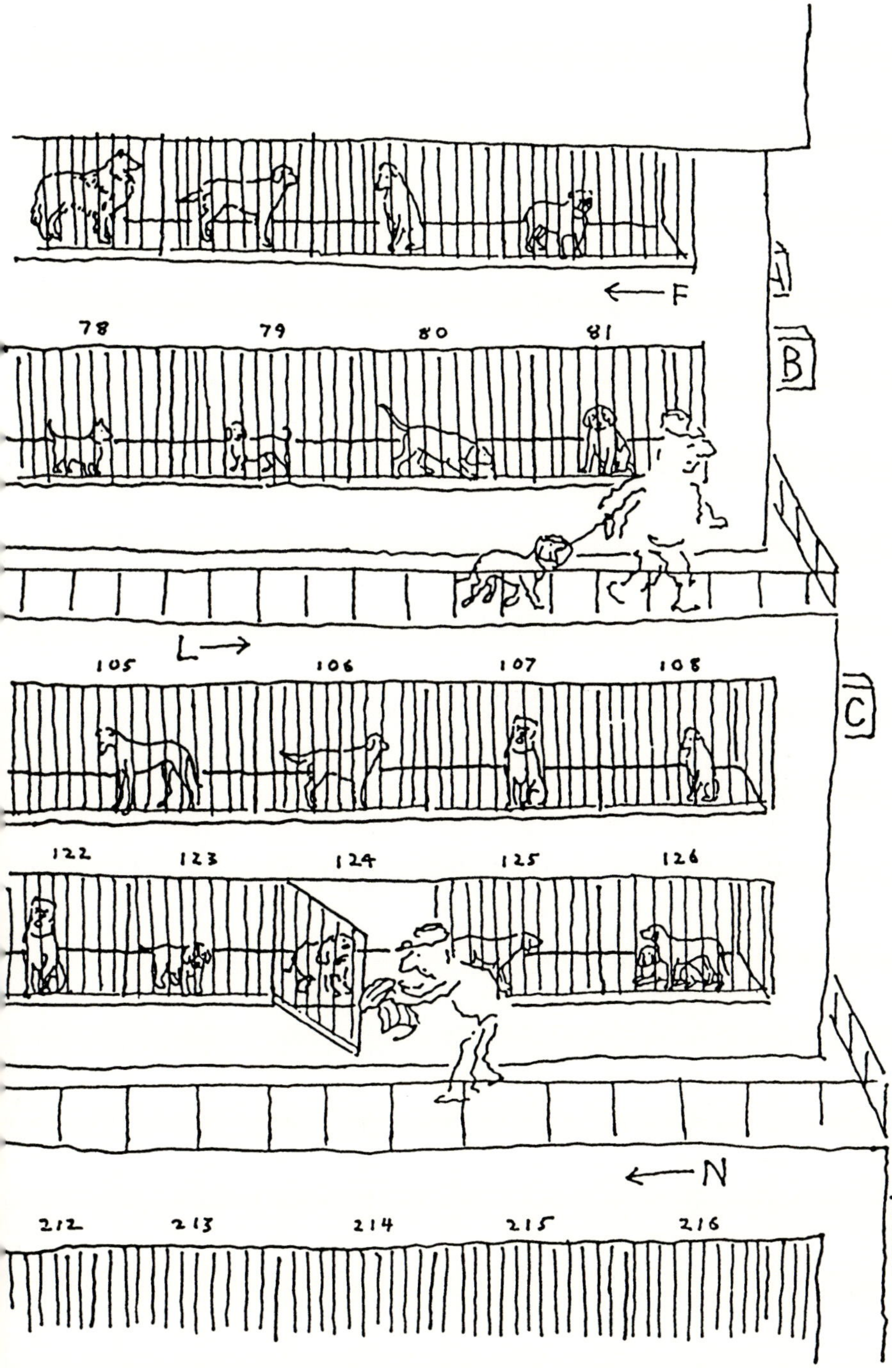

← F
78
79
80
81
B
L →
105
106
107
108
C
122
123
124
125
126
← N
212
213
214
215
216
D

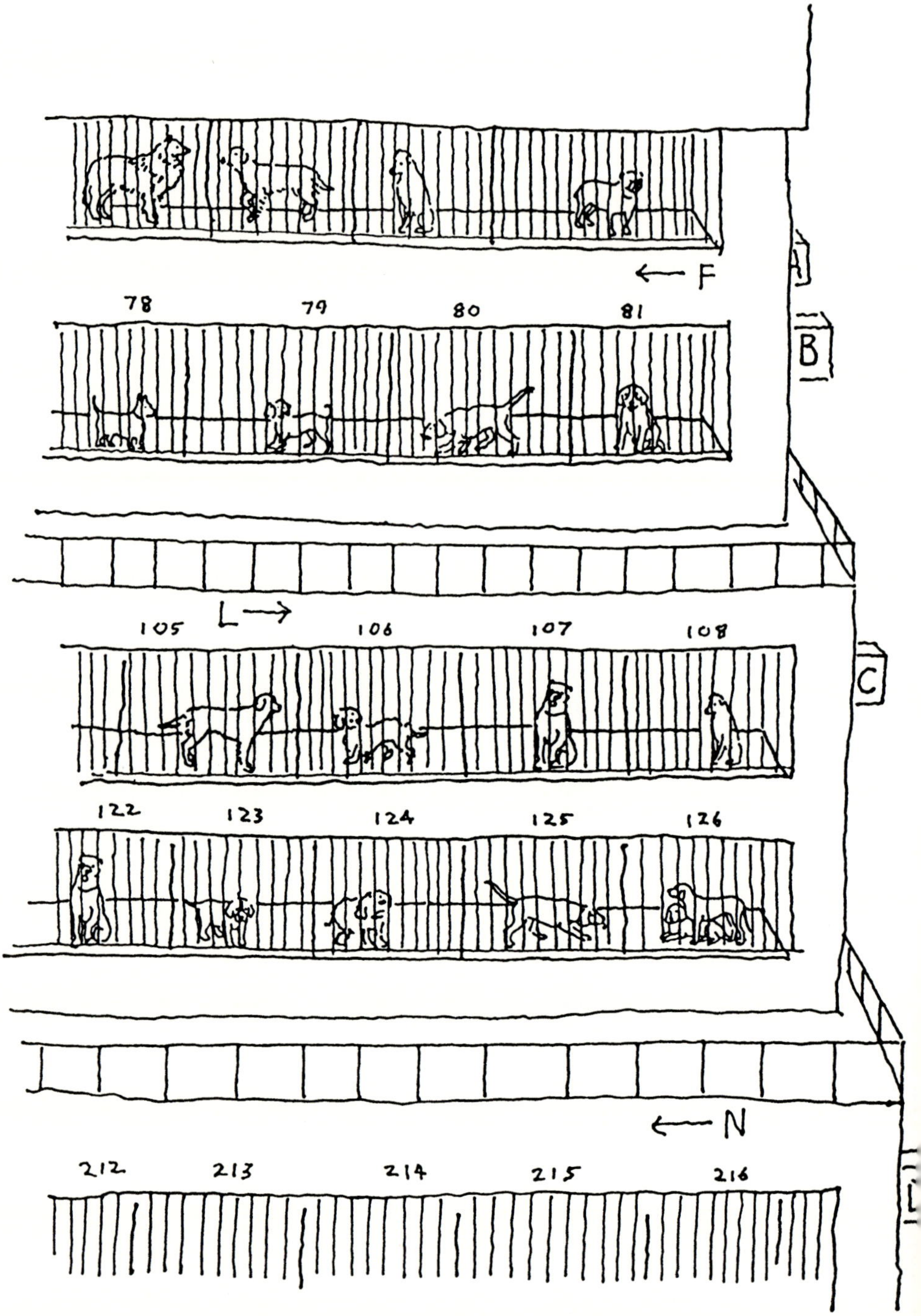
F
78
79
80
81
A
B
L
105
106
107
108
C
122
123
124
125
126
N
212
213
214
215
216

124

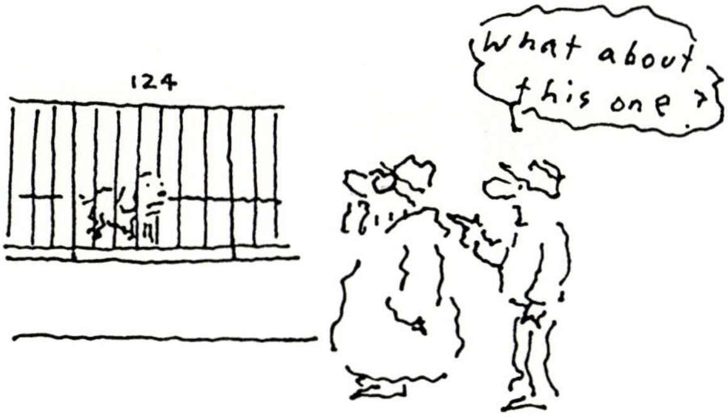
124
What about this one?

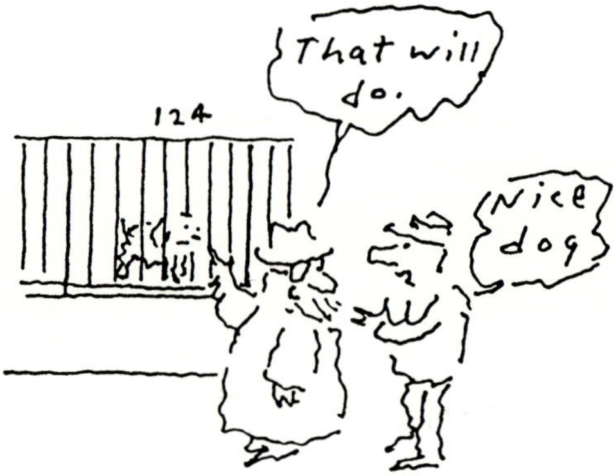
124
That will do.
Nice dog

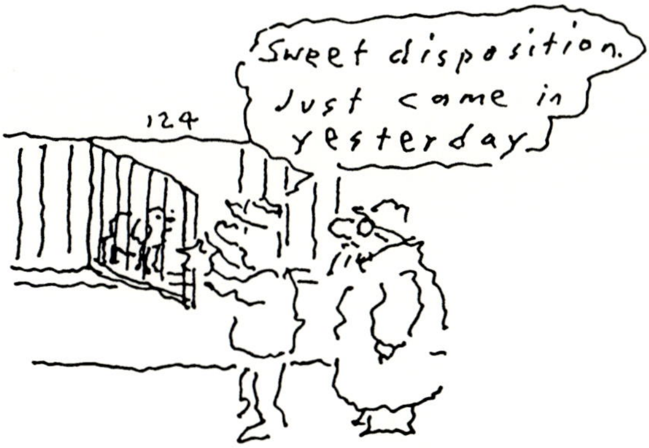
124
Sweet disposition. Just came in yesterday.

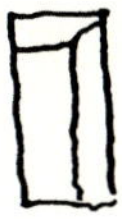

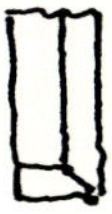

Hello,
Georgie.

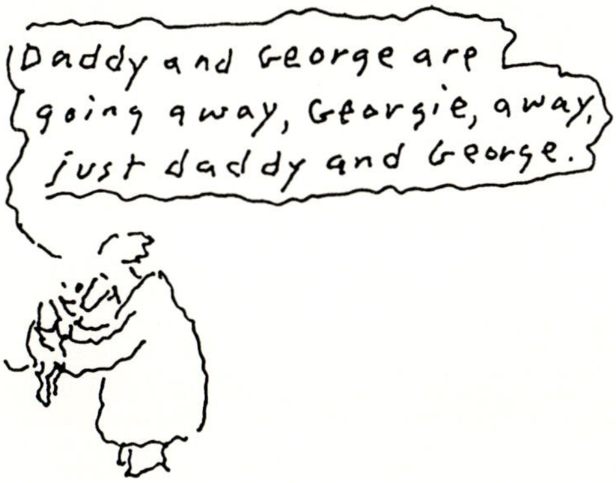
Daddy and George are going away, Georgie, away, just daddy and George.

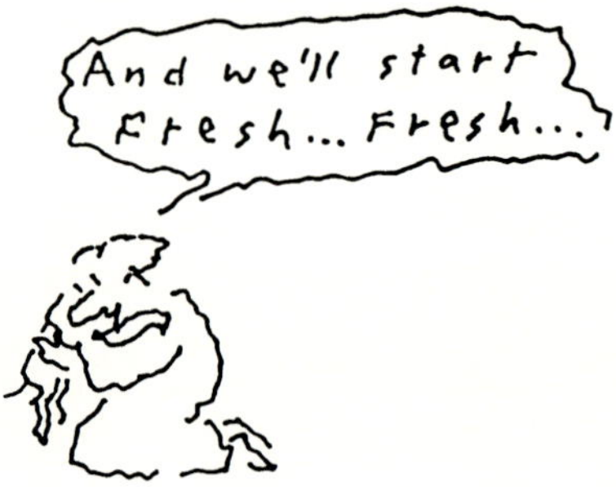
And we'll start fresh... fresh...

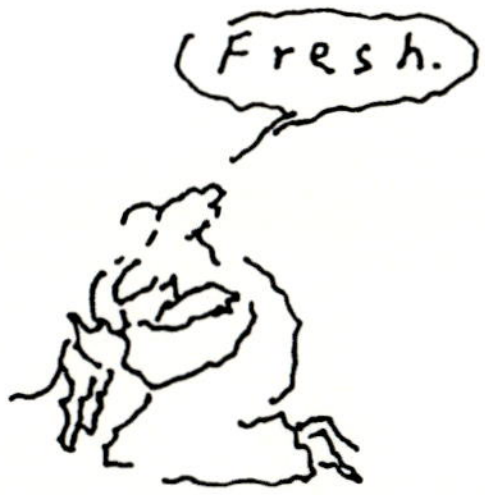
Fresh.